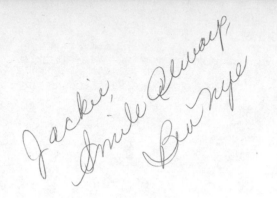

A Family Raised on Rainbows

A Family Raised on Rainbows

by

Beverly K. Nye

Book design and illustrations by Tom Dusterberg

Writer's Digest Books
Cincinnati, Ohio

Published by Writer's Digest Books, 9933 Alliance Road, Cincinnati, Ohio 45242.
SECOND PRINTING, 1979

Library of Congress Cataloging in Publication Data
Nye, Beverly K., 1934-
         A family raised on rainbows.
1. Home economics.   2. Handicraft. I. Title.
TX145.N9   640   79-14261
ISBN 0-911654-71-2

Dedicated to

Kim Christiansen — who married our Stephen May 1, 1978

Mark Seethaler — who married our Kristen May 2, 1978

and Bruce Barrett — who married our Heidi July 13, 1979

They have brought such special rays of Sunshine and warm smiles into our family. May they, with their new mates, build Rainbows of cherished memories for their eternal families.

Acknowledgments

Many, many thanks and bunches of love to my husband Roy for the patience, love, understanding and encouragement he has given me while working on this manuscript, and to our children who have worked to make this a family project—

Kristen — for her diligent typing of the manuscript

Mark — for his painstaking work on the index

and Kim, Stephen, and Heidi — for their long hours helping with the mail.

Thanks, too, to my viewers of "Sunshine Corner" on the Bob Braun Show for their patience in getting recipes and answers to their letters,

and to my many friends who have shared ideas, helps, and encouragement for this book.

And, again most of all, I wish to thank my Heavenly Father for helping me to express the things that are in my heart.

Contents

Introduction IX

1. A House Becomes a Home 1

2. Beauty for a Song 15

3. A Stitch in Time 25

4. Sweet Little Pinks and Blues 39

5. Over the River and Through the Woods 61

6. A Handful of Green Thumbs 75

7. Happy Days Called Holidays 93

8. The Year-Round Gift of Christmas 111

9. Tradition! Tradition! 131

10. Your Own Special Rainbow: Keeping It Bright 147

Index 161

Introduction

Hi! It's so nice to be back visiting with you again. I've made so many choice friends through *A Family Raised on Sunshine*. It was fun sharing my recipes and family food ideas and I've really enjoyed and appreciated all the great ideas and recipes I have received from you. This is what makes homemaking so rewarding. There are always new ideas to share.

Being a wife, mother, and homemaker is a big challenge but isn't it fun to wear so many hats, so to speak, and have such a diversified life? There isn't another occupation or calling that could help us grow in so many fields (nor be nearly so satisfying).

In my *Sunshine* book I shared with you how we have raised our family to good health by eating properly. Tasty foods and well-planned meals *will* bring brightness and sunshine into your family life, but that is just the beginning. In this book I would like to share all the rich colors in the rainbow of our family life; from gardening, sewing, and hobbies to holidays, traditions, and family outings. Just as the rainbow is a revelation of the unexpectedly glorious ingredients of ordinary light, this book will help you transform everyday occasions into sparkling and memorable moments. These will grow into a sense of family togetherness that will *keep* the magic of the rainbow in your home.

We have tried to bring up our children with these family-enriching things, not only to make the most of the fleeting moments of daily life but to build for the future. There is a real pot of gold at the end of this rainbow, one you can pass on to your children and they to theirs — the experience of a warm, strong, and joyous family unit.

1
A House Becomes a Home

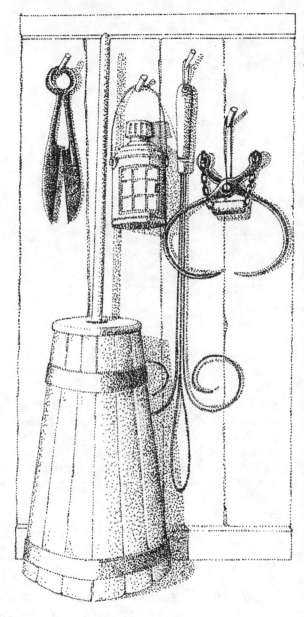

Our surroundings play such a big part in our physical and mental well-being that one of our biggest roles as homemakers is to make our homes comfortable and attractive. Notice I mention *comfortable* first, because that is what should really be our prime concern. Our homes should be a secure and cozy refuge from the outside world—a place where our families feel warm and happy and where they want to bring their friends to share that warmth. I'm afraid this is a lesson that took me a while to learn. When Roy and I were first married, I worked so hard at keeping the house pretty that I forgot the word *comfortable*. I guess that really hit home when I noticed Roy walking *around* the shag rugs so he didn't make a footprint on them. I have to admit it's pretty bad when you can't walk on the throw rugs! I decided right then and there that I had to change my ways and keep a home that he felt comfortable in. It's surprising how much happier that change made both of us. It reminds me of a saying a friend once told me when I was upset with Roy for being late coming home for dinner and my meal was getting over done. She said, "You're having a meal for your husband, not a husband for your meal." The same goes for a home, and how much more content I've been since I've realized this. After my change of attitude, our house really became a home for all the family members. When it becomes "our home" instead of "my house" everyone becomes involved in making it a prettier and more loving place. Furniture is chosen with everyone's likes and comforts considered, and the decorating is done with everyone's interests, needs, and hobbies in mind.

We are all very much interested in history, which brought about our love of antiques. We have spent many enjoyable hours roaming the countryside and exploring junk shops for antique pieces. It's been a real education for all of us. We try to collect useful things, and our specialty is primitives. As we find an old butter churn, rug beater, sheep shears, or ice tongs, it's fun to discuss with the kids the ways the original owners probably used them (and, of course, throw in a few "I remember when..." stories). The real fun part is to hear the kids show off our treasures and repeat our stories to their friends when they visit our home.

We try to display our collectibles in a natural setting and, when possible, even use them in our daily routines. Roy loves to sit by the fire at night and read by his favorite antique oil lamp. It is a double-wick variety and was made in England (the home of his ancestors), so he is extra proud of it. The ticking of the old school clock hanging on our wall is always so soothing and somehow reminds me how precious each ticking minute is. Our collection of crocks is used as wastebaskets throughout the house, and a special one holds my cooking utensils near the range. I also have quite a few old canning jars; you know, the blue glass type with a zinc lid. They are the nicest containers on my counter top for things like cornmeal, rice, oats, etc., and they look so pretty, too.

I try to have candles in every room, not only because they are practical (the electricity does go off occasionally), but, next to bread baking in the oven, nothing else gives such a homey feeling as glowing candles. Ask a local florist to save the used candles for you after he has done a wedding. You'd be surprised how many candles are accumulated and wasted this way. I have several large boxes of white tapers that have only been burnt an inch or so. Just remember to be sure and use them in a safe way. Keep them a good distance from anything flammable such as drapes, cushions, dried arrangements, etc., and out of the reach of small children.

We have used the antique and primitive furniture we've found to furnish our entire house. It's not only good as an investment (this is one type of furniture that is worth more every morning you wake up), but it also gives our home a warm, comfortable feeling. Those nicks and scars just add character to the wood, and you can almost hear it telling you the story of its life. I have a big old pine china cupboard that I'm especially fond of. I'm sure it's had quite a life. Why, it even has an old tin can lid nailed over a mouse hole in the back! I love it!

As we have stumbled on to these rare finds, many of them have needed to be redone. If it has a missing part, such as a knob or drawer pull, be sure and keep looking at old junk and furniture stores for a matching part. Many of these stores have boxes of pieces and parts. They are intriguing to look through and you often find just what you are looking for. If you don't *have* to, never put new hardware or parts on an old collectible. It can really distract from the beauty of the piece.

Be especially careful if the piece you find is a genuine antique (over one hundred years old). It could be truly valuable, and much of the value can be destroyed if you strip off the original finish, replace a part with new materials, or change it in any way. With something of great age, it is always safest to just clean it well until you get an expert's opinion. Check with a reputable antique dealer in your area. Otherwise, you are ready to begin a fun adventure in furniture refinishing.

With some trial and error, we have found this procedure to be the best, and it gives a beautiful, hard-wearing finish. First, if the piece is loose or wobbly, we take it apart and work on it piece by piece. Otherwise, you can just do the whole thing at once (as long as it is good and sturdy). The first step is to completely strip it with a water-soluble stripper. Work with the direction of the wood grain and do only a small area at a time. Make sure it is well stripped and then, rub it down with fine steel wool, again in the direction of the grain. Next, clean it well with a damp cloth and seal the raw wood with a sealer. We use shellac. After this has completely dried, rub it down good again with fine steel wool to take away the shine and smooth the finish. Last, apply a good three or four coats of paste wax and rub it well. Natural wood has such a pretty tone and glow, I hate to cover it with any kind of stain; of course, this is a personal preference.

Keep your eye open for an antique or family collectible, and I'm sure it will start you on your way down memory lane with us. Already our two married children have started furnishing their first homes with items of meaningful memories.

It may be an item that you used as a child and has special memories, such as the old egg basket you gathered eggs in, a picture exactly like the one you remember hanging on your Grandmother's wall or maybe a syrup bucket like your Daddy carried his lunch in as he walked down the road to the country school.

Wall decor is also an area where your family's creativity can go to work. Have you ever done tin art? It is so fun, and it dates back to the seventeenth century. Start with a board; I usually use a scrap of pine. A piece of 1-x-6 inch lumber cut the length you desire makes a good size to start on. Many lumber yards will even give you scraps of boards they have cut. Stain and varnish it. (Before we do this we like to "antique" it by pounding a few nails into it on an angle to simulate worm holes and then bang it up a bit to give an aged effect. I even take a knife and whittle on the edges to give it a worn look.) After the varnish is completely dry, cut a piece of tin (I use sheet metal) and tape a picture drawn on paper to the front of your piece of metal. I use pictures out of a simple coloring book or something that has a very simple outline. Then with a nail and hammer, just start outlining the picture. The secret to authenticity is that you follow tradition and use an uneven number of types of nails and screws so that you get several variations of holes in your picture. For example, make three holes with a big nail, seven with a smaller nail, etc. When your picture is finished, mount the piece of tin to the board with a small nail in each corner. Then just finish it off with a little antique-finished ring on top. You can really be creative with these by using different types of objects to make holes and a variety of pictures. Just remember that simple pictures work best and, to make them just like the pioneers did, use an uneven number of nail and screw shapes and sizes.

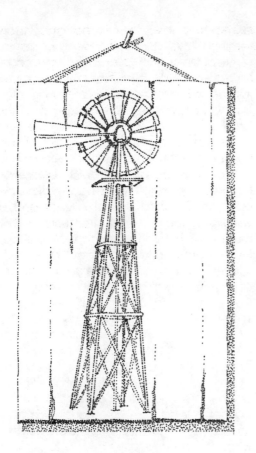

originally used a hot iron from the big fireplace.) After you have well burned the outline into the wood, you are ready to add a touch of color. Now again, to be authentic, use only white. The original shingle artists used only whitewash to highlight; so, white is all I use, too. These pictures served as wall hangings as well as for advertising such things as "eggs for sale," etc. Try some of these. They can be very versatile and are a fun conversation piece.

For people like me with a poor memory, every home needs a birthday calendar. They add a pretty touch to a wall and also serve as a reminder of family birthdays. To make these, I buy a heavy canvas or duck material in a cream color. About 16-x-20 inches makes a nice size. Then, I hem the sides or use bias tape. Put a hem across the top so you can run a dowel or rod through, and then finish the bottom with fringe or just a hem. At the top is written the family name, such as: "The Nye Family" or "Birthdays at the Nyes'" or "Who's Who at the Nyes." I write this with a permanent black felt-tip marking pen. A few flowers bordering the title or a little decoration adds to the top. Then we mark it off in twelve squares, one for each month, again with the felt-tip pen. Each box is lettered with the name of the month on top, and then the birthdays are filled in. This way, any new additions can easily be listed. For example: under the month November, we write *11-Heidi*. If you like to embroider, it's fun to add little monthly motifs on each corner, such as a little red heart in the border of February. However, I'm not the most patient embroiderer, so I either leave that to Kristen, my oldest daughter, or I cut

We also like to do shingle art because it lends a warm, primitive feeling to our home and because it really is an art form from the past. To do this you begin with a wooden roof shingle of any size. A simple picture is drawn or traced on the shingle. Be sure and use a very simple picture. I like to choose things depicting an earlier era or rural feeling—a butter churn, pitcher, a loaf of homemade bread, an old barn or a lantern, a windmill, etc. Then you trace the outline of the picture with a child's wood-burning tool. (Of course, the colonists out little colorful felt things and glue them on the corner of each month; a horn and hat or clock for January, hearts for February, a shamrock for March, raindrops for April, flowers for May, a tree for June, firecracker or a flag for July, a big sun for August, a bunch of fall leaves for September, a pumpkin for October, a turkey for November, and Christmas tree for December. The calendar is so pretty when it's

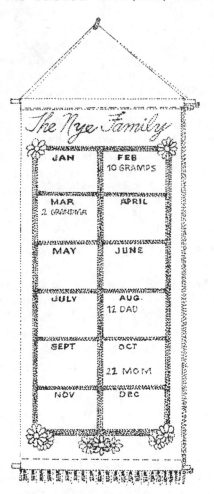

The Nye Family

JAN	FEB 10 GRAMPS
MAR 2 GRANDMA	APRIL
MAY	JUNE
JULY	AUG. 12 DAD
SEPT	OCT 22 MOM
NOV	DEC

completed and serves as a constant reminder. I think everyone likes to be remembered with a card or note on his birthday. A little personally written note is just as much or even more appreciated than an expensive, store-bought greeting card.

We have always taken slides at our house since the kids were little, so we don't have a lot of photographs to browse through or show off to company. Because each one in our family had a favorite slide, we picked these out, had them printed into photographs, and made a wall gallery. I just bought the standard black document frames to hang them in. The grouping starts at one end with the grandparents, then Roy and I as children, and then several shots of each of our kids as they were growing up. It ends with their graduation pictures. We now have a narrow wall gallery of wedding pictures, also, and plan the next wall for our grandchildren (of course!). This has always been a special part of our home. Even though we have moved a lot, the first thing we decide is where to put our gallery!

As you decorate your home, you don't always have to use just wall hangings. Get brave and "Beautify" a whole wall! One of our boys' favorite rooms was in Texas. We painted three walls a pale blue, then on the fourth wall we used maps that we had saved from the *National Geographic* magazine. The whole wall was "wallpapered" with maps. Of course, the boys chose maps that were significant to them. They put big red stars and markers on places like Kansas City, Omaha, Salt Lake City, and Plano (Texas) where we had lived. They also highlighted places they wanted to go, such as Germany and France. It was lots of fun (and educational) for them. By the way, we just hung them with regular wallpaper paste. Since they were different-sized maps, we all had fun putting them up and fitting them together. Almost like a jigsaw puzzle! Travel posters or animal posters would also be good for a child's room.

Wallpaper stores almost always have a bin of "sample" or overstock rolls of wallpaper. Check these often; you can make a room very pretty and interesting by papering just one section, maybe behind a book shelf, a corner seating arrangement or a wall of plants. A wall is also a great place to display collectibles such as menus from traveling, picture post cards, posters, or signs. A grouping of these things can be a real conversation starter.

We always keep our eyes open for new wall decor. Things turn up in the most unusual places! We found our most talked about one in a glorified junkyard in Kansas City. It is the one end off an old treadle sewing machine stand! In a large design it has the word *Household* (the brand name) worked into the wrought iron. We just formed the name *Nye* from strips of wood, painted it black like the wrought iron, and inserted it above the word "Household." We now have the cleverest large wrought iron sign hanging next to our front door that says "NYE HOUSEHOLD." It never fails to bring a comment from a visitor.

One of the prettiest things I've seen is in the home of our friends, John and Virginia Rowe in Kansas City. They, too, discovered it while "junking." It is a piece off of the base of an old organ, down just above the pedals, and it's a beautiful piece of carving. They simply stripped it and waxed it well, and it really makes an elegant hanging. Since Virginia is a fantastic organist, it makes a very appropriate piece in their home.

Every home needs a place set aside to reflect the talents and abilities of the family. It might be a complete wall, a bulletin board, or even a cupboard or refrigerator door, but, whenever guests enter, they know that there is love and pride from each family member in that spot. You could display clippings from the paper about Dad's advancement; pictures of that beautiful duck or pheasant he got on his last hunting trip; a copy of that special poem Grandma wrote to the family; or that blue ribbon Mom won for her apple pie at the county fair. How special it makes little ones feel to have their artwork displayed. Who knows, you may have a budding artist on your hands! Our second son, Mark, turned out to be quite good with oil painting. When he expressed talent and interest, we enrolled him with a private teacher. (After a family council, we decided to start up our little bakery route again to provide him with the funds and opportunity to develop his talent.) He took lessons for several years and, during high school, he earned money by teaching lessons at our home. We have some very special works he has done that we feel add a unique touch to our home.

Creativity never ends when it comes to making a house a home. Love and originality is expressed in so many ways. Have fun with your ideas.

Throw rugs on the floor add a warm and comfortable feeling to a home also, and these can be your own creation. Our family really got excited about making carpet-scrap rugs. These are so simple, they wear like iron, and you can really use your imagination. Almost any large carpet store or laying company will give you their trimming scraps. Getting scraps can be quite an experience in itself. You should have seen us practically hanging by our feet in those big metal garbage bins behind the carpet stores digging out the scraps!

After you have gathered a good supply of a variety of colors and textures, you are ready to start. Small scraps make the prettiest designs. Don't plan a design with pieces too large or it will cheapen the appearance of your rug. Try to keep each piece small in relationship to your finished rug. You will want a heavy piece of canvas, duck or denim in a little larger size than you want the finished rug. First, I mark a two-inch border all around the edge with a marking pen. This will be turned under *after* you finish the rug and will serve as a hem. Start cutting your scraps into desired sizes and shapes. It works best to cut carpet scraps on the wrong side with a razor blade cutter, using a wide board to cut on.

I lay out my pattern before I start to glue. This way I can decide if I want a random patchwork style or a definite picture. We made a rug for my niece, Judy, that was a white shaggy lamb on green background. Then we added a few colorful flowers. Our favorite was a tiny patchwork for my sister, Maxine (the pieces were only about three or four inches square). It was made from those little swatches out of a salesman's sample book. I have also seen a big shaggy lion that was really cute (squirrels,

raccoons, or kittens would be good subjects, too); a circle rug with pie-shaped wedge pieces, a scene using white shag scraps for clouds etc., stripes in different shades of one color or even the family monogram set in a solid color. We usually stick to patchwork, though, since it goes with our "antique-y" look. You can really get some pretty color combinations.

After you get your pieces cut, just apply a carpet adhesive to the back side; I use a little scrap piece of carpet to put it on with. Then just stick the piece of carpet on to the backing fabric. As you fit each piece together, be sure that you hold the yarns of the carpet so that you can butt each piece up tight to the last one—especially if it's a thick pile weave. After all of the pieces are glued on, apply glue to the back side of the hem, turn it under, miter the corners, and you have a neatly finished piece.

Making these rugs almost becomes a fetish. You won't want to stop and it is so easy and fun. One of my friends, Marge Reeve (Emery) in Kansas City, did her whole bedroom, wall to wall. You sure can't beat it for being inexpensive. And pretty, too! To clean, just use any carpet cleaner, but don't get them too wet with the cleaning solution.

I've been making another type rug now that I'm really excited about. I guess because I hate to waste a thing, I have finally found a great use for those double-knit scraps I have left from sewing.

Cut a piece of heavy denim (or something similar) such as lightweight canvas, duck cloth, or heavy poplin in a rectangle the size you want the rug. Next, either hem the edges or bind them with bias tape. Then cut polyester double-knit scraps into

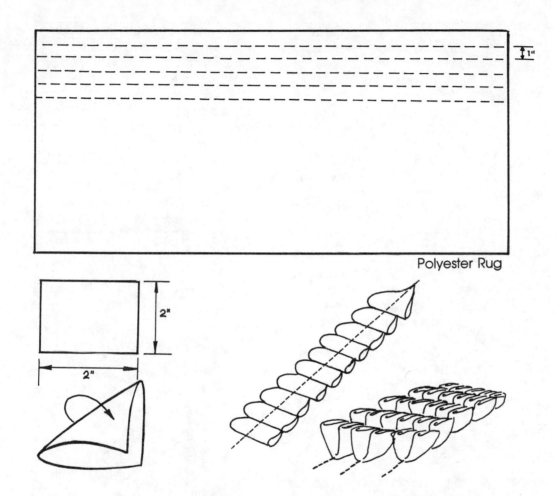

Polyester Rug

two-inch squares. I don't really measure—I just cut a long strip and then snip it into *about* two-inch squares. After you get a whole bunch cut (and it takes a *whole* bunch), you are ready to begin. I usually have a sack or basket of scraps handy and, when I'm stuck on the phone for a long time or when I just need to sit down and rest a few minutes, I cut a bunch of squares and put them into my plastic bag.

Now to actually start on the rug. After you have finished hemming the border, take a ball-point pen and draw lines one inch apart down the full length of the fabric. Then you're ready to go to your sewing machine. Fold the little squares over into a triangle with the points toward you, place the first one on the pen line, and start sewing. Overlap each triangle about halfway over the last one, and you can just

10 "zip" down a row as fast as you can feed the little folded triangles under the pressure foot. When you start to sew the next row, just fold back the protruding side of the first row of triangles out of the way so that you are able to sew the centers of these triangles right down the middle of the new line. Repeat with each row and soon all the triangle edges will be standing up to form a nice, thick rug. (This explanation may sound a little confusing, but it only takes a minute to get the hang of it, and it sews up so fast. I love making them.)

These rugs are so nice and thick and comfortable to have by the kitchen sink or the back door. They wash and dry like a dream, and you can't wear them out.

Now, you just can't overlook sheets for decorating. You can't begin to buy fabric for the price at which you can get a sheet. Of all the houses we have lived in, I don't believe there has been one in which I didn't make some curtains from sheets. Just hem the top and bottom, gather it onto a rod, and you can have cute little dainty prints for a bedroom, bright cheery ones for the kitchen, elegant ones for a living room. The fabric is heavy enough that if the curtains are gathered on your curtain rod you can just slide them shut at night, and you don't have to buy window shades.

Sometimes I trim the plain ones with ball fringe or tie them back on each side with a wide ribbon. You can't beat it for being easy, and yet they have so much more personality than ready-made curtains. I always manage to have some extra left over, so I make toss pillows for the bed, a dresser scarf edged in lace, a little skirt for a round bedside table, or even a little set of pictures for a grouping.

For these pictures, I just buy some more of those inexpensive document frames and cover the cardboard in the frame with my little print fabric. I cut a special picture of a family member or relative in an oval shape and put it in the center of the fabric. Then I finish the oval edge of the picture with rickrack to match and put the picture in the glass frame. It really gives a custom look to your room.

No scrap is too little to save. I even make little pincushions and personal items to match and accessorize the bedroom. (We'll talk more about that in Chapters 3 and 7.) Do watch those sheet sales, though. There is a lot more potential in them than just making a bed.

If you've read my first book, *A Family Raised on Sunshine*, you'll know that I spend a good deal of my time in the kitchen, so I like to personalize that room, too. I especially like my spice jars. I collected a whole bunch of baby-food jars from friends (bouillon cube jars work well, too). Then Roy nailed the lids up under the front edge of my cupboards where I do my baking. I made little labels by cutting masking tape with pinking shears and printing the name of each spice on the tape pieces. I just fill my jars and screw them off and on with a touch when I use a spice. It is so handy—they are always available. I can see which ones are getting low, and I'm reminded to use ones I may forget about if they were out of sight. A touch of spice can really put life into a dish.

Another reason this works especially well is that I buy all of my spices and seasonings in the one-pound commercial-size cans from the bakery supply company or food wholesalers. This is a good idea if you use up grocery-store size containers of spice as fast as I do. Just look in your Yellow Pages under *Wholesale Grocers* or *Wholesale Bakery Suppliers*. You'll be astonished at the savings. If one can or box is just too big for you, you can always split with a neighbor or friend and both save. Just remember to keep your big can of chili powder, paprika or other red spice in the freezer, because they will get "buggy" if

they sit out too long. Also, ground spices lose their flavor more quickly than non-ground.

We like to use place mats and cloth napkins at our house. Remember my telling you to save your permanent-press scraps and hem them up for napkins in *A Family Raised on Sunshine*? It's such a nice feeling to have a cloth napkin, and very few people like paper ones. To make place mats, I watch for specials on quilted fabric and then I buy a bunch or even just a remnant. To make a pattern, just cut one out of newspaper by tracing around an old place mat that you already have. I put two pieces together back to back and stitch them together on the sewing machine in a quilting design. Sometimes I just follow the lines already stitched in the quilting. After they are stitched together, I bind the edges in a solid color bias tape or make a self ruffle. If I use the solid color for the binding, I can use the same solid color for making the napkins. Sometimes I'm even lucky and find matching print *un*-quilted fabric and can make matching napkins. These sets make such nice gifts, especially for a bridal shower (although some of us could use a bridal shower again after twenty-five years, right?). Compared to the retail cost of place mats and napkins, you can really do a lot for pennies.

Getting the mail is always a highlight in everyone's day at our house; so we have had lots of fun with our mail bag. Again I used scraps, this time from upholstery pieces. I made a bag with six pockets. The upholstery piece I used for the top was out of a sample book. It already had two metal holes in it, so it worked very well to

12 hang it from two cup hooks in the wall. Each person's pocket had his name printed on it in large letters. Then, when I got the mail each day, everyone's was deposited in the right pocket. The fun part was that it soon got used for many other things: a special little note to cheer someone up on a rough day, an "I love you," a reminder, and sometimes an apology. That little mail bag proved to be one of the most used items around the house.

Many of my ideas and helps have come from our monthly Homemaking Day at Relief Society, which is the women's organization of the Mormon church. It is such a fun day because we learn helpful things in all phases of homemaking, and it gives us a chance to share ideas with one another. Keep your eyes and ears open to new ideas always. Just a friendly little visit with a neighbor can spark an idea and send me on my way down a new path of endeavor. It's surprising, too, how many good ideas our husbands and children come up with if we just listen. Our oldest son, Stephen, has always been our efficiency expert, and hardly a day went by that he couldn't offer an easier and simpler method for us to do something. "Out of the mouths of babes" — we can learn so much from them.

If we as homemakers always remember that it is "our home" and not "my house," we can really create a little heaven on earth.

2
Beauty for a Song

"To dream of the person you would like to be is to waste the person you are," someone once said. There are so many beautiful people in the world, and you are one of them. Today, just stop for a few minutes, count your blessings, and list all of your good qualities. I'm serious. You are a pretty special person and you have to believe in yourself. Nothing can help us to grow and accomplish things more than a feeling of self-worth. To build with determination is the Lord's way. You have to like *you* in order to like others. To like ourselves doesn't mean to be all puffed up with pride but to have a peaceful feeling within that gives us the determination to do all we can. Then build on your successes.

Well, I didn't mean to preach, but I really feel strongly about having a positive attitude. It can certainly make a big difference in everything we do and become.

Everyone wants to feel good, and the first place to start is with appearance. I learned a long time ago that if I'm careless about how I look, it affects *everything!* — my thoughts, mood, attitude, even how I physically feel and things I accomplish. You don't have to be wealthy and own a fabulous wardrobe; you really can have beauty for a "song."

I begin as soon as I wake up in the morning by stretching every part of me. That gets the blood circulating, and I know I'm alive. Then I try always to start each day by showering, putting on a little makeup, and touching up my hair, and by wearing something comfortable yet neat and appropriate for what I plan to be doing for the day. We should take just as much care choosing our clothes for everyday at home

as we do to attend a special event. After all, we are executives managing our homes, and nothing makes it harder to concentrate or work than something that binds, twists or is ill-fitting.

The same, if not more so, goes for shoes. Boy, what a difference good-fitting shoes make! My kids tease me sometimes about my "health" shoes, but I just tell them, "Better those than a frowning face!"

When you get up tomorrow, try my little routine and see what a difference it makes. It sure beats an extra hour's sleep. It's like that old saying, "An hour lost in the morning has to be chased all day." I promise you the best day you've had for a long time.

It took me a long time to realize the value in wearing an apron, but I couldn't get along without one now. It saves so much on the laundry, and I can just slip it off and look fresh and clean. Maybe you aren't as messy as I am, but when I'm cooking, everything sure has a way of getting all over me, too. Just be sure your aprons are made of nice washable fabric and are a practical style (see Chapter 3). Lots of aprons are made for looks only and really don't do too much "protecting."

I always have a little mirror hanging in my kitchen so that if someone comes to the door or my husband comes home, I can take a quick peek and brush that flour off my cheek or straighten my hair. If you have children at home, even if they are small, they too, appreciate your looking nice. It gives them a calm, peaceful feeling, and somehow we always wear a happier face when we look nice. Remember the story of the little boy who was feeling sad because his mother was grouchy? He went out the

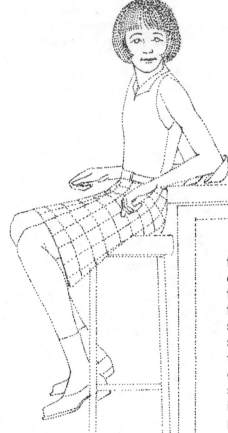

to have such beautiful complexions, and one reason why is that they spent a lot of time stirring a steaming kettle. All the while they stirred, that steam was purifying their skin. Then, as they became hot, they would splash cold water on their faces to cool off, thus closing the pores. Presto! A pretty, glowing face. So next time you are standing at your stove stirring that steaming kettle, take advantage of it and get prettier at the same time.

One of the first things I learned about beauty from the kitchen was when I was a little girl. I had those typical "little kid grimy elbows." So, mom would cut a lemon in half, squeeze out the juice, and then have me sit with my elbows in those lemon rinds. I suppose I looked pretty silly sitting there with my elbows in those lemons, but it's amazing what a bleaching effect it has. It really works!

Speaking of lemon rinds, I always keep a plastic bag in my refrigerator where I put

back door, around to the front, and rang the bell. When his mother came, he said, "Hi, mommy! I was hoping you'd have on your 'company' face!" Remember the importance of a *smile!*

Since we spend so much of our time in the kitchen, there are many beauty aids right there that we might as well take advantage of. Let's start with that steaming kettle on the stove. Our grandmothers used lemon, orange, and grapefruit rinds. Then when I've had a rough day and would like a leisurely soak in a nice tub, I just turn on the hot water and throw the citrus rinds into the tub. Golly, it makes the water feel so soft and the scent is terrific. I almost feel like Cleopatra!

Occasionally I save the orange rinds and lay them out on a paper towel to dry. When they are dry and hard, I make little 3-x-6 inch cloth bags with a drawstring out of scraps of fabric and fill them with the dried orange rinds and cinnamon sticks. I stuff a bag in each of my shoes in the closet and it keeps them smelling so nice. Every so often I give the bag a squeeze to scrunch the rinds up a little more, and they last a long time.

Rolled oats are a great beauty booster, too. I keep a wide-mouth container of oats near my sink. After working in the garden, peeling fruits and vegetables for canning, or whatever, I just stick my hand in the jar of dry oats and rub it around. It keeps my fingers nice and white and sure has a softening effect on your cuticles. I also make another little drawstring bag about 6-x-6 inches of washable cotton or terry cloth, and fill it with four tablespoons rolled oats and some dry crushed mint leaves or other spice (such as basil, lavender, crushed cinnamon stick, or sage). This I use as a rub in the bathtub. It really gives your skin a nice soft feeling. It lasts a long time and makes a nice little gift, too. How about making some to give away with this little note. "Here's a little bath bag, filled with oats and spice. Next time you're in the tub, your skin will feel so nice."

Our youngest daughter, Heidi, found rolled oats to be the best skin cleanser there was when she was a young teen-ager. She just put about one-half cup of oats into the blender and ground it fine. Then each morning and night she would mix a small amount with water in the palm of her hand and scrub her face. It really cleans the pores and works wonders.

We all get that plain tired feeling when our eyes look a little puffy. Well, next time that happens to you, pour a little milk into a dish, and let it come to room temperature. Then soak two cotton pads in it. Squeeze them out and apply them to your eyes while you lay down for ten minutes and put your feet up. It sure does help. A few fresh cucumber slices laid on your face for about ten minutes while you rest serves as a great astringent.

I hope you are keeping a bag of celery and carrot sticks clean and ready to eat in the fridge (see *A Family Raised on Sunshine*). It's great for those tired times, too. When you feel like you want a snack, they are right there. Also, the chewing action is good exercise for that double chin. A piece of fresh fruit serves the same purpose. And, when you peel that orange, don't pick off all the white membrane. It is one of the best things you can eat for healthy gums.

Please don't overlook the benefits of a good, healthy, balanced diet on your beauty as well as on how you feel. You can do it! If you eat a proper balanced diet, you don't have to buy expensive vitamins. Remember a balanced diet consists of:

Milk group—adults—two or more cups,
children—three or more
Meat group—two or more servings per
day; this includes nuts,

dried beans, eggs, etc.
Vegetables and Fruits—four or more servings per day; always include citrus and green leafy vegetables

Bread and Cereals—four servings per day

You know, that old "copout" that diet foods are more expensive is just hogwash. Skim milk is less costly and just as nutritious as whole. Fish and poultry are cheaper than beef. The organ meats—liver, heart, etc.—contain more important minerals and are less expensive than steaks or chops. Whole grain cooked cereals do a lot more for you and cost a whole lot less than the cold commercial kind. Cutting down on all the convenience and junk foods cuts our budget and helps our health. Those fresh fruits and vegetables in season can't be beat. Soon you'll be feeling so much better and so righteous! I know you can do it! Just don't go on any "far out" diets. Sooner or later you are going to have to return to normal food, and then it's so easy to gain all of that weight back. Just start good eating habits now.

One of the most basic beauty aides for the whole family is soap. Stephen, our oldest son, came up with a good money saver. We just melt down some paraffin or some old candle stubs and dip one side of our bars of soap in it. Then, we let it harden. This eliminates that gooey soap jelly on the sink and tub and makes our soap last twice as long.

It's so much fun thinking of ways we can look prettier by using things that we have around the house. I guess I learned this from my Grandma Benson. She was such a clever and inventive person and always looked like a million dollars. I used to sit for hours listening to her tell me of the creative things young people did then. Eating carrots was supposed to make your eyes sparkle, and they always chewed a few fresh mint leaves to keep their breath "kissing sweet." My favorite story was how they used a little flour to take away the shine on their noses and a little beet juice to put some color in their cheeks. I still smile when I think of her getting all "prettied" up!

We couldn't think of getting prettier without including exercise. I even put my kitchen to work in this area. It seems like my stomach muscles are the ones that need the most tightening all of the time. So, as I stand at my sink or range, I play a little game by holding my stomach taut for the count of ten and then relaxing and doing this over and over. Sometimes I do this as I wash dishes; hold my stomach tight while I wash a dish, relax while I rinse it, then tight while I wash the next one and so on. I even do this as I'm driving the car. I hold my stomach taut as a car passes and then relax it until the next car (being careful to watch my driving, of course). You'd be surprised how much this helps if you do it regularly

When my phone rings (and it seems like it does quite often), I sit on the floor with my back to the wall and my legs extended. Then, I draw one knee up and slap it down on the floor. I do each leg this way several times while I'm on the phone, and it really helps to keep the inches off of those upper thighs. Of course, I try not to huff and puff into the phone! Maybe you'd better start out by just doing it when your best friends call.

One of the exercises I enjoy most is washing windows. It's great for those flabby upper arms. Besides, nothing cheers you up and "brightens" your outlook like shiny windows. Remember my inexpensive window cleaner, too. Just take a pint squirt bottle, add four tablespoons rubbing alcohol, four tablespoons plain, old, household ammonia, and fill it up with water! It works fantastically!

I also use my plastic milk jugs as weights to do my evening exercises. I can fill them with water to make them as heavy as I want. Try it—they're free!

Speaking of my evening exercises, I've found that the best way to succeed at this is to get your husband or one of your children to do it with you. Husbands are really more fun, but sometimes they are a little harder to motivate. When I first started, Heidi did them with me. She really thought it was a riot when I did the "jumping jacks." Sometimes we'd be laughing so hard we'd have to quit. But remember, a good laugh never hurt anyone either. It does wonders for your facial muscles (and your heart). I soon had Roy doing them, too, and I can't begin to tell you how much better we have felt in so many ways. We each worked up a little routine for ourselves concentrating on the areas we thought needed the most work. We found the best time for us was right before we had family prayer and went to bed. However, you might enjoy it more in the morning. Just enjoy it, whenever. Don't make it *work*. Laugh a little and have fun.

Besides our exercise program at night, we also enjoy walking. I think this is one of the most therapeutic things we do. When we were first married and living in a *very* small apartment, it always seemed easier to go for a walk to discuss our problems or ideas than to sit in that little confined area. It has just become a habit with us and our kids have picked it up, too. I've had many a choice conversation with the kids while we went on a walk together. Somehow the words flow more freely as you are walking in the clear air. I hope you'll invite someone for a walk tonight.

To become more beautiful, we have to exercise our minds as well as our bodies. They say, "Beauty is only skin deep," but don't you believe it. No one is more beautiful than the person who has a peaceful yet vibrant spirit. This great, big beautiful world is so neat, and there is so much to learn about. We should be filling our minds with uplifting things constantly. I've always said that if I lived to be three hundred, I could never get bored because there is so much to learn about. Don't you agree? We should never feel that something is too complex or difficult for us to study or read about. Let's expand our minds just like our lungs. There's really lots of space in there we can still fill! Our knowledge and intelligence is really all we ever keep with us and we do want to be good company for ourselves as well as for others. Try learning a new word each week to increase your vocabulary (and just for the price of a dictionary!). Learn more about someone else's occupation. Start with your husbands! Nothing is more flattering to him than to have you be genuinely and intelligently interested in what he does. (Does wonders for your marriage, too!)

One of the best places to expand your mind is the public library. Imagine the wealth of material there for free. One of our favorite family night activities when all the children were home was to walk to the library together to spend an hour. On our way home, everyone shared visions of what they were going to be or where they were going, via books, that week. The options were unlimited.

After you have exercised your physical body tonight, ask yourself how you have exercised your mind. What have you learned today? Tomorrow decide to learn two things!

Nothing brings a prettier glow to your face than to make someone else happy. This can be done for a "song," also. You don't need to spend a lot of money to bring happiness to someone. Giving of ourselves is the most beautiful gift of all.

Let me share with you a gift I recently gave my husband. I got this idea from a friend of mine, Douglas Brinley, director of an institute of religion in Ogden, Utah. It is an inexpensive little apothecary-type jar with a ribbon around it and a label on the front, saying:

Roy's Happiness Notes—from Bev
These notes are guaranteed to uplift, encourage, and please you. To be drawn at the rate of one per week.

1. Good for an evening attending any sports event you'd like, together.
2. Good for one special moonlight walk together.
3. Good for a dessert of your choice.
4. Good for one extra-special backrub.
5. Good for a movie of your choice.
6. Good for writing two letters for you (he hates letter writing).

7. Good for a quiet evening reading your favorite book. (I promise not to bother you.)

8. Good for a nice polish on all your shoes.

9. Good for a romantic evening together. (If I'm not in the mood, you'd better put it back and draw again!☺)

10. Good for a special big kiss.

11. Good for an evening at the symphony (he loves this).

12. Good for a nice big hug and I Love You from the heart.

The list goes on and on. Give one to your someone special. Just remember to give him the things that make *him* happiest. Sometimes we get carried away with our own creative ideas that we forget the gift is for someone else. Think of their needs, desires, and wishes so that the gift will be personally "for them." This, in turn, will give you the most joy.

The most successful beauty tip in the world that is absolutely free is to smile always and have a positive attitude. So let's put our lives in order and develop a feeling of contentment. Here are just a few rules to follow:

1. Simplify your life. Don't let nonessentials push away the things that bring true happiness—your husband, family, and basic convictions.

2. Do one thing at a time. I have a little saying over my kitchen sink that says, "You can only peel one potato at a time." Accept this and it sure helps give you peace of mind.

3. Be patient with yourself and others. Don't expect the impossible from anyone, especially yourself. Learn to laugh at yourself and your silly mistakes. It makes you much easier to live with, and you'll feel better, too.

4. Control your thoughts. Only you can do this, and you can think about anything *you* desire. Push out negative things, substitute a funny saying, a song, or just a pleasant mental picture. Learn to *think* happy.

5. Enjoy today. Don't waste it worrying about yesterday or dreading tomorrow. This day will pass quickly. Do something to build rich memories.

6. Take care of yourself. This is *your* responsibility. Exercise regularly. Think healthy, and your body and emotions will follow the pattern.

7. Roll with the punches. No one is going to have a trouble-free life, but use your troubles as stepping stones and learn from them. If you don't have what you think it takes to make you happy, then be thankful for what you have. There is always someone not as blessed as you.

8. Praise others sincerely. Let *your* accomplishments speak for themselves. Don't worry about gossip—just live your life so that nobody believes it.

9. Be a good example for your children. Your actions, not your words, are their first teacher.

10. Determine to be happy and enjoy what you have. Once you take this step, you'll be the richest and prettiest person there is.

3
A
Stitch
in
Time

Have you ever looked at the price tag on a garment, hanging on a rack in a store and then glanced in the mirror at the much prettier one you have on that cost only a third the amount? If so, you know the feeling of joy and satisfaction you get by creating something you can be proud of. If not, please let me encourage you to pick up that needle and give it a try. Sewing is like cooking. It isn't a talent you must be born with. It's easy to learn, and the more you sew the better you become. Begin by realizing that you won't turn out perfect results every time, but learn from your mistakes—have fun, smile, and go on. Life won't come to an end, and you get better with each try.

The one rule of thumb I would always go by is to be simple. A very simple skirt, well done, is so much more becoming than a very complicated one "botched up" that won't look good on you and then will discourage you from trying again. As you become more aware of style and design in good clothes, you will soon notice that the simple things are the most elegant, while the contrived or fancy things are usually a cheaper line of clothing.

Let me tell you, the day you finish your first well-done sewing project, you will feel ten feet tall and experience a wonderful sense of pride and satisfaction. It really gives you confidence, just like that first successful pretty pie you baked.

Sewing can really become a skilled craft for you, so just like in any other craft be sure you start with a few pieces of good equipment. Can you imagine a good carpenter building a house by sawing the boards with a toybox handsaw? You don't need to spend lots of money on nonessen-

tials, but be sure your sewing machine is in good working order. Lots of shops run specials on cleaning and oiling machines. Call your nearest dealer and ask him when they will be having one. Be sure you have a pair of sharp scissors (and, here again, sharpening specials are always available), a good supply of pins and needles (both regular and ballpoint size and type really make a difference here), a tape measure, a yardstick, an ironing board and iron, and good lighting (this is crucial).

Before I begin to sew, I always take a little brown paper sack (lunch bag size), roll it down a little at the top so that it stands open, and tape it to the end of my machine. I have learned over the years and through the classes I have taught that nothing makes a person more nervous while sewing than to be in a constant *mess*. All those threads and scraps piling up around you can really be a bother. With my little sack handy, I can just brush the scraps into it. Somehow we never seem to hit a wastebasket, even if it's sitting close by! With my little sack handy, I can just brush the scraps into it.

In making a garment for ourselves (or someone else), there are several important things to consider that are as vital as the sewing itself. First, we have to decide on style, color, and type of fabric. I have a little trick here that I started while I was doing lots of sewing for my two daughters and myself. We would go shopping at some of the nicer stores in town (being sure we wore dressy shoes, good undergarments, and had our hair fixed attractively so that we could see how we would look in new clothes). We would then select and try on things that appealed to us. It didn't take

28 long to tell that certain styles or colors weren't for us. When we found a particular "look" or color that we felt was attractive, we either made a sketch of it in our notebook or just in our mind's eye, and then we would leave and head for the discount fabric store. This little idea has sure saved many dollars and much time, because sometimes we think we would like a special style, but when we see it made up on us it is quite a different story.

When you get to the fabric store, your pattern should be your first choice. Remember to keep it simple, to be sure (and honest) about your measurements, and to consider if the design is a good one for you. (If you have previously tried on similar clothes, you will know this.) Avoid lots of ruffles and frills if you are very heavy and tight narrow things if you are tall and thin. Play up your good features. A softly gored skirt and tailored collar is flattering on nearly everyone. Necklines make a big difference in your appearance, as well as sleeve types.

Once I find a good basic pattern that fits me well, I really stick to it and use it many times by exchanging a sleeve or collar piece to change the look a little. Be sure and note any changes on the pattern envelope so that each time you use it, you remember to add two inches at the waist, length, or whatever.

Then you are ready to select material. There are several rules you should follow here, too. First, never buy fabric in a store without a full-length mirror. Unroll the fabric several turns and hold it right up to your face. It's amazing what different colors or even shades of a color can do for or against you. Then be sure and read the end of the bolt. Not only does this tell you price per yard, it also gives you width of fabric, content of fabric (man-made or natural, cotton/polyester, linen, wool, etc.) and laundry instructions. This can make a big difference in your selections, as I'll explain. Then I always give each fabric the old "hand" test. I grip a little part of the fabric in my sweaty little hand and squeeze hard. I let go, and if it wrinkles badly, I know that choice is not for me. Now last and very important, is the fabric compatible with the pattern you chose? If the pattern has lots of pieces, you certainly wouldn't want a big, bold plaid, huge flowers, or a large design. If it is a full flowing garment, you wouldn't want a stiff or heavy fabric, etc. Keep in mind the weight of the fabric and when you'll be wearing it. Also, the care and upkeep is important. Will it be practical? Remember, "keep it simple." The nice part about keeping it simple is that a well-fitted, well-made simple garment will not get "dated"—a tailored shirt or an A-line skirt can always be dressed up or down with a scarf, belt, jewelry, etc. to look in style. If you are willing to invest your time, labor, and money, make it worthwhile!

Before you begin to sew, be sure you check your pattern pieces for measurements (sleeve length, waist, and skirt length, etc.) Don't ever start cutting until you are sure of each piece. Also, be sure and prewash all fabric (and trim) that you plan to launder after the garment is made. Even though many fabrics are now labeled "preshrunk," it's possible they could "shrink" a bit, and what a shame it would be after spending all your time and money if the garment wouldn't fit after it was washed. There is also a residue on all knits and permanent-pressed fabric that should be washed out before sewing on them. If not, they can be very hard on your machine.

Before you begin cutting the fabric, be careful to match stripes and plaids. Nothing looks worse than a plaid dress or skirt made of a plaid that is totally off right down the back or front. Be aware, too, of one-way nap such as corduroy, suede, and velvet. If one side of your skirt is going one way and the other side another, the two sides can look like a totally different color. I've made a couple of boo-boos like this is making pants in my younger years. I wore them around the house anyway, and Roy joked that he couldn't tell if I was coming or going! My worst boo-boo happened when I was laboring over a very special party dress for days. I loved the dress, wore it to the party proudly, and wore it many times after until I finally noticed one panel in the skirt back was upside down (with the print). I was so embarrassed! And I always thought I looked so nice in that dress, too. Darn! I've been a lot more careful since then!

The most important part of the construction of your garment is the cutting out. Be sure your selvages match, your design or plaid matches, your pieces are running the right way, and that each piece is on the straight of the grain. This can make a fantastic difference in how your finished piece hangs.

Never, never cut out with a pair of pinking shears. This can throw you off on seam allowance so much, and your finished product could be way too tight or loose. This is a place where it doesn't pay to try and save time. If seams need pinking, do it after you have stitched the seam.

Be sure and transfer all markings to the fabric piece. It's much easier now than later. I use a tailor's chalk or pencil. The neatest way to mark a dart is by making a tiny snip on the fabric edge at each side line of the dart and one in the center line. Be sure you just make a tiny snip and don't cut beyond the seam allowance. Then mark the point of the dart (on the wrong side). To sew the dart, you don't even need pins or basting. Just fold the dart matching the snips, and it'll fold automatically on the center snip. Start sewing at the *outer* snip, holding the point of the dart in the other hand, and stitch right to the point and *off the material!* This is important. Never stop stitching on a dart before you get to the point or you will have a little dimple at the end. Sew from the wide end of the dart to the point and right off the fabric!

As you begin to sew, it is a *must* that you always use a five-eighth inch seam so that your fit comes out as planned. If you don't have a marker on your machine, just put a strip of masking tape along five-eighths of an inch out from the hole where the needle goes down. This way you can just guide your fabric along and know you are getting a true five-eighth inch seam.

Along with that strip of tape, another little gem that I have working for me at my machine is my little pincushion. I just took a couple of plain (*not soaped*) steel wool pads and made a little square covering to stuff them in. Then I sewed the end shut. I also sewed a loop of elastic on this so I could secure it around the top arm of my machine. This way it is sitting there right in front of me, and pins don't get scattered all over. The steel wool is also great for keeping the pins sharp!

The next absolute rule is to have your ironing board set up and handy. Every seam should be pressed open as you sew. This is a must if you want a professional look. Without pressing, you will get a frumpy "homemade" look. This is especially true if one seam is going to cross over another at an intersection, such as at the neck or underarm. Where this is taking place, diagonally trim the corner end off of the seam to eliminate bulk in the intersection. Stay stitching is really important when it is called for, especially around neck or waist openings. It eliminates stretching, and you could have a really ill-fitting item without it.

Darts are the key part of the bodice of a garment. Be sure when you check your pattern pieces, before beginning, that the bust darts are properly positioned. Nothing looks funnier than having a dart two or three inches above or below your natural bustline. When pressing your darts, never press beyond the point or you will get an unbecoming fold. A rule of thumb for direction of pressing darts is always press down or in toward center. So when you are in doubt which direction to press, just remember "down or in."

In sewing a skirt, remember two things. First, as you sew any seam always sew in the direction of wide to narrow (which, in the case of skirts, is nearly always from the bottom of the skirt to the top). Second, if gathering is called for, try my neat way. It guarantees uniform, perfect gathers every time. We've all had experiences with gathers that were kinda hit and miss. You know — a bunch, then a long gap and then

a few more gathers; or worse yet, gathering a skirt to a bodice only to find you've caught a big piece of the skirt up into the gathering line. Well, these things will never happen when you use this gathering method. Whenever the directions call for a gathering stitch, make your first row of wide stitching one-fourth inch from the edge of the fabric. Then make your next row just under five-eighth inch from the edge. Now make a *third* stitching about one and one-half inch from the edge of the fabric. Pull all *three* bobbin thread ends together at the same time, as you gather, and space your gathering equally. Then sew your seam together as directed. After the garment is completed, remove the third row of gathering stitches. You'll be so pleased. It will have held all the gathers in place, and they will be as even as the smocking on a baby's dress, with no more hunks and gaps in gathering. This has really been a help to me.

Sleeves are the next major part of constructing a garment. As you cut out the sleeve, be sure you make a little snip at the center top marking and also the side notches. It is really important that these notches match the ones in the armhole of the dress. This distributes the fullness properly so that your sleeve doesn't pull. Also be sure you always put the double notches in the back and the single ones in the front. This is a standard rule with patterns that many people don't realize. Whether it's a bodice piece, sleeve, or skirt panel, double notches are for back and single for front.

Here is a nice, quick, and easy hem for a plain, short sleeve (the type used on a man's short-sleeved shirt) that is fun to use

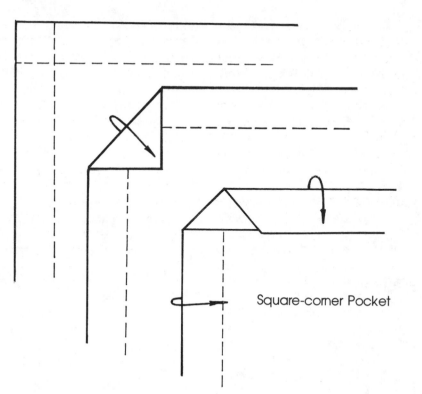

Square-corner Pocket

and can also be used on the hem of pants. Turn under amount desired for cuff appearance (usually about one inch for sleeves and one and a half for pants), press well, then turn the same amount under again and press. Now stitch a row of machine stitching one-fourth inch from the bottom edge. After you have finished stitching, pull down from underneath the folded section. No raw edges will be exposed, you have a nice finished cuff appearance, and it doesn't require any extra fabric allowance. I especially like this finish for children's clothes because it seems that they are always having a hem come undone.

Heidi and I both have a thing about pockets and love to have them on everything we make. There is a trick to a nice square-cornered pocket, too. After your pocket is cut out, stitch five-eighth inch from the edge clear down each side and off the ends, then clear across the bottom and off the edges. Turn under one-fourth inch and stitch across the top. Fold top to outside about one inch and stitch across the ends. Trim the little seams and turn right side out. Then *press* each bottom corner up on an angle as you would wrap a package, folding right at the intersection of your stitching. Then fold up each side and across the bottom, and you'll have a perfectly mitered corner with no raw ends showing. It works great. Then just double stitch your pocket to your garment, and you'll have a very professional-looking pocket.

The one important part of a collar is the point. Have you ever done a collar that ended up with two little nubbies on the ends? This is a dead give away for a homemade garment. To avoid this, be sure you cut off the points of your interfacing before stitching it to the collar. Then as you stitch the collar, stitch right off the ends across the back and down the sides. This will give you a true point and makes sure that both sides match. After that step be sure and trim the points well before turning to eliminate any bulk.

Just a word or two about sewing on buttons. If you are sewing them on children's clothes or where they will get a lot of wear, just double or even triple your thread before you thread your needle. That way you get two or three times as much strength with a single stitch of the needle. If you are sewing a button on something heavy, be sure you allow some give between the button and the fabric so the buttonhole lays nicely and doesn't pucker. To do this, take one stitch through your button and slide a straight pin through the stitch and across the top of the button. Then continue sewing over the pin. After the button is sewn on, slip out the pin and you'll have some slack in your button. This really helps give a professional look when the garment is buttoned.

A pretty, little, different touch can be accomplished by using a self-covered button. Before cutting out the circles of fabric to cover the button pieces, draw

Blind Hem

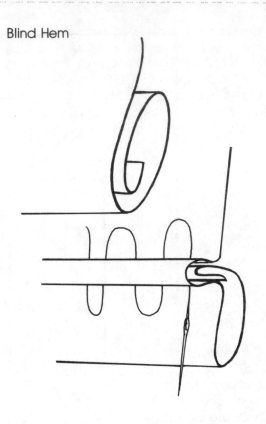

your circles and embroider little flowers, initials, or designs in each circle. Then cut out and apply the circle to the button shank. They look so pretty and give a personal touch.

The final thing to be done on any garment is the hem. It is usually a good idea if you can let the item hang on a sturdy hanger at least overnight before hemming. This gives the fabric a chance to hang by the weight, and you will get a truer hem marking. Now, when you are ready to mark your hem, be sure and put on the shoes you will be wearing with it and have someone mark it for you. Stand straight and tall and have *them* move around *you*.

We are all built differently and hems need to be even. Keep in mind that a normal hem should always be between one and a half and two inches to look proper. A little skinny hem or a huge wide one is just another "give away" shouting home-made. The only exception to this is when you are using a special type of fabric. A sheer dotted swiss or organdy looks nice with a three- or four-inch hem and some soft, silky or tissuey types lend themselves to a tiny rolled hem. Again, check the nicer stores and see what the experts use.

In doing a regular hem, we finish the edge by using a hem tape or lace or just stitching under one-fourth inch of fabric. When you do this, stitch along the *outer* edge instead of the inner raw edge. It will be neater than just turning up one and one-half to two inches and stitching with a running hem stitch. I never buy regular hem lace. I watch for sales on laces and trims and buy yards and yards of tiny lace. It is so much cheaper and I think it works better because it is softer.

When hemming knit fabrics, never finish off the raw edges; they can be pinked if you like, but even that isn't necessary. In fact, it often looks neater and more professional if it is a straight edge. Just turn your hem allowance up and stitch with a very *loose*, free-flowing stitch. Remember, it should be able to "give" as your fabric stretches when you sit down or walk. If you stitch too tightly or secure a stitch, your dress will pull and pucker. Be sure and steam press all hems from the wrong side by lifting and pressing—never slide your iron along the fabric.

After using your talent and skill to make beautiful clothes, care is really important.

We can make our clothing budget go even further if we take the proper care of things. I'm so thankful for my clothesline because I love to hang my things out to air before I press them. It really helps. Proper hangers also make a big difference. I like to keep a supply of padded ones so that I don't get little "peakies" on the shoulders of my knit dresses and tops.

These hangers are simple to make. I watch for a special and buy ones with a wooden cross piece. I cover the wooden part well with scraps of quilt batting. Then I sew two tubes of calico print fabric and slide them on each end, meeting at the center where the hook is connected. To make the two tubes, cut four strips of fabric two and one-half inches wide and fourteen inches long. Put right sides together and stitch down both sides and across one end. Then turn right sides out. After you slide them on the hanger ends, whip the center seams together. Depending on how much batting you wrap on the hanger, you may want to top stitch a little edge down each side before slipping the fabric on the hanger. These can be done in bright prints to match your bedroom and finished off with a little bow. They can also be made to match the shoe-bags and other things in Chapter 2. You'll find you have the prettiest closet.

My sewing room is a treasure full of goodies. Start now by saving bits of everything, and you'll soon be surprised at the nice gifts you can make for nothing. I take plastic leaf bags and label them to keep my leftover fabrics. That way all the wools are together, cottons, quilteds, knits, felt, etc., and it's so easy to find what I want. I also save all zippers, buttons, snaps, and useable trims when they reach the "rag bag" stage. With the price of buttons now, why throw away all those nice ones because the shirt is no longer wearable? It's amazing what uses you'll soon have for even a little leftover yarn, so start now with containers or bags for everything.

I love to work with tricot knit. It is so simple to sew with, and I can whip up matching half slips for all my outfits with *very* little cost and no effort. Try making one for yourself and see how simple it is. Tricot comes in really wide pieces so you can get lots for little.

To make a half slip, first cut off the selvage edges. (It has dots of hardener on it to keep it from rolling up.) Then cut two pieces (front and back) the length you want your slip. For the width, take your hip measurement plus three inches. Divide that in half and cut each piece that wide. At the top of each piece, cut, tapering down about five inches, starting in about one inch. Set your machine on a tiny, close-together zigzag stitch. Sew *one* side seam, sewing about one-fourth inch from the edge. This little excess will be trimmed away later next to the stitching, but it's easier as you begin working with tricot not to try stitching right on the edge (this can be done later as you become more adept). After you sew one side seam, seam your lace at the bottom, again with the zigzag stitch. You can either put the lace right at the bottom or have the tricot fabric under the lace. I prefer the second way because I feel the lace wears better. If the lace is wide, stitch along the top and bottom edges trimming away excess tricot at the bottom. If you use a little pair of scissors you can trim *right* next to your zigzag stitching. Now sew up the other side seam, enclosing lace in the seam also. Remember, stitch wide to narrow (or bottom top) in the side seams.

The last step is to put on the elastic. This is such a neat way, I just love it. I use this method on knit pants, too, and they lay so nice and smooth. It doesn't give me a "gunny-sack-tied-in-the middle" look like casing elastic can. Cut a piece of elastic your waist measurement *minus* four inches and stitch ends together with zigzag. Mark the elastic in even quarters. Mark the slip in even quarters (side seams, front, and back). Pin the elastic to the slip only at the four quarter points having the elastic on the wrong side of the fabric, top edge of fabric and elastic even. With a wide running zigzag stitch from quarter point to quarter point, stitch along the *bottom* edge of the elastic, stretching it to fit each quarter of fabric. Then trim away the top of the tricot above the stitching, turn elastic to right side, pinning again at quarter points, and stitch with running zigzag along the bottom of the elastic stretching the elastic as you go. It works great, and it really looks nice. When I do this on slacks, I start with the elastic on the outside of the fabric so that it ends up on the inside. You'll be so pleased with how they fit. If you want to try knit slacks like this just use your regular well-fitting pattern, cut to include the darts but don't stitch them. Eliminate the waist band and placket. Just stitch up the seams and add the elastic. It's so easy! When you see how fun it is working with these things, you'll be making beautiful nighties and everything with knit and especially tricot. You don't even need much of a seam—just use your zigzag. You can always just use laces to

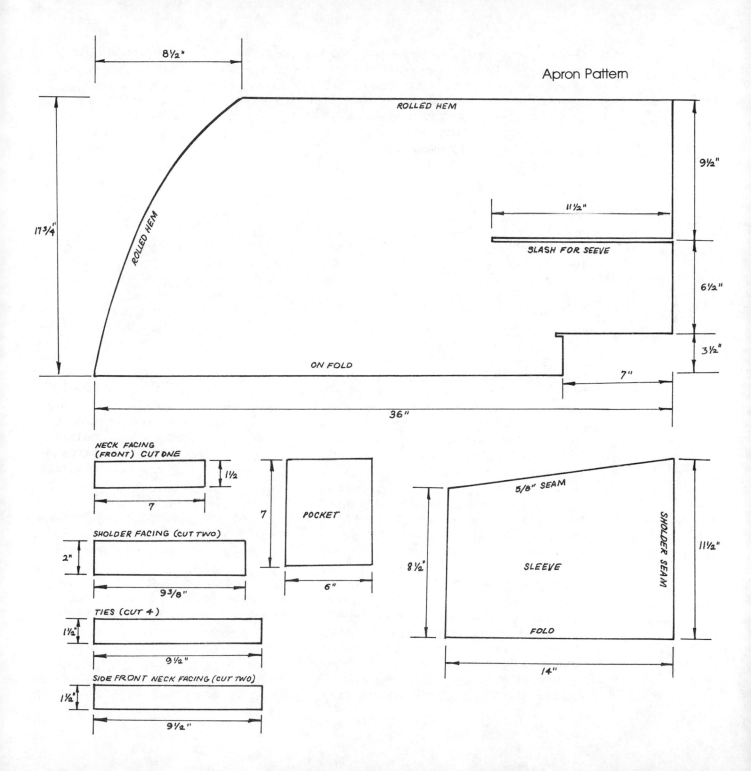

Apron Pattern

finish off edges around sleeves or the bottom of a gown. No hemming! It's terrific, and you'll look like a million. I'll have to confess, nightgowns are my weakness. Heidi always teases me about making another nightgown, but I can feel so luxurious for such a few pennies. It's good for my ego!

We can't look frivolous all the time, though, and the work does have to get done, so let me share with you my favorite apron pattern. I get so many requests and comments on these aprons when I wear them on television, so I hope you enjoy it. As I have said, I'm kind of a messy cook, and this apron even covers up my arms. I love it!

Aprons are really a blessing, and I don't know anyone that can't use one. I have fun creating different looks with this pattern, and my girls are always voting for the one they want. These are also a good beginning sewing project for kids. They can be anything from very tailored or oriental-looking to really fussy and frilly. Just use your imagination.

Speaking of the girls' sewing, I have to share with you an idea they really get a kick out of. You know how you can buy the cut-out figures in the fabric stores to make stuffed toys out of, such as cartoon characters, Santa Clauses, Raggedy Anns, or the Seven Dwarfs. Well, we cut them out, leaving an ample border two to three inches and then make the cutest T-shirts or sleep shirts. Slide a large piece of cardboard between the front and back of the shirt, then pin the front of the character on the front of the shirt and his back side on the back of the shirt. Then again with a tiny close-together zigzag stitch, stitch all around the black outline of the character.

When you have finished stitching, use a little scissors and trim the excess fabric away next to the stitch. It's so much fun to wear these shirts—you can see them coming and going. The little ones love this idea, using the Santa at Christmas sewed to their PJs. It makes a fun gift, too.

Since I do so much sewing, I do wear out ironing board pads and covers pretty often, so I have to tell you about another of my waste-not, want-not ideas. You know, the one end of your ironing board pad hardly ever shows wear as much as the other (the middle and the other end are "shot!"). Well, since they are heat resistant and flame retardent, I use the good parts as filler to make hot pads. Just cut the good pieces into squares or circles and cover them with some pretty scraps of fabric. Then stitch a big X across it to hold the layers together, and you have the greatest hot pads ever. Sometimes, if I have a pretty big piece, I even get fancy and make a mitt. Just trace around your hand for a pattern. Allow ample material for fit.

Since I spend so much time in my sewing room, I like it to be decorated as nicely as any other room or area in my house. One of my pictures I got from a treasure handed down to me from my Grandma Scheel. As a child she had embroidered a turkey-foot design in many colors on a piece of pillow ticking. This was then stretched into a wooden embroidery hoop which I have varnished and tied with a little bow through the wire spring on the hoop. I have done several hangings like this. Embroidery hoops lend themselves as picture frames so easily and can be painted bright colors, black for colonial, or even just varnished. There are so many pretty print fabrics that can be used. These are especially cute hung in a series in a baby's room with some of the children's fabrics available now.

So don't be hesitant to pick up that needle and thread and try your hand at creating. You may enjoy it so much that you'll get done with your chores twice as fast so you can get back to your sewing machine.

Smiles and Happy Sewing!

4
Sweet Little Pinks and Blues

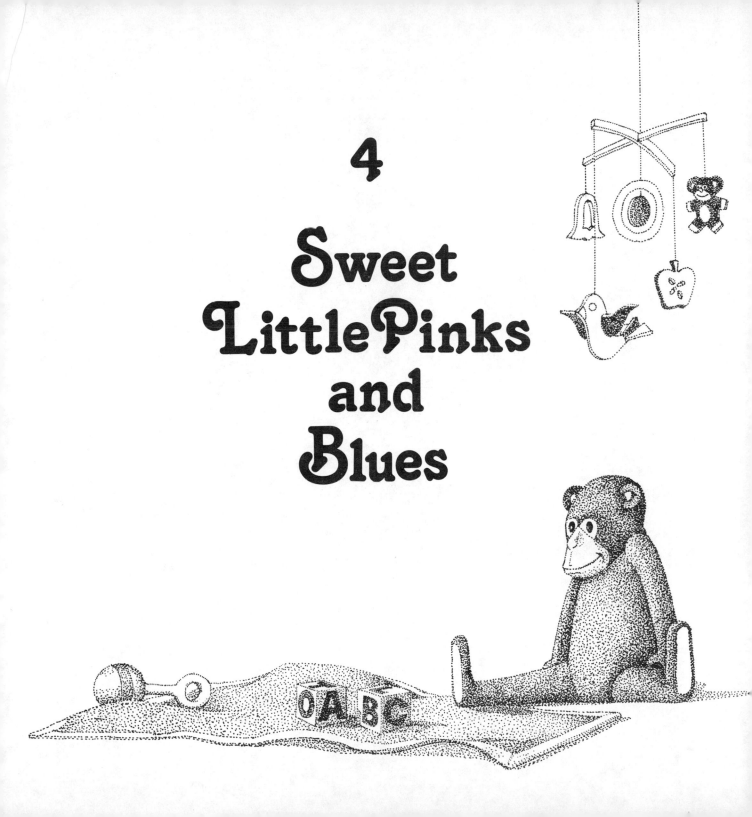

This is a great time for me to talk about little ones. We just got a phone call from our son, Stephen, and his wife, Kim, telling us we are grandparents for the first time! It's a little girl, Emily Marie (eight pounds, five ounces), and we are about to "bust our buttons." And our daughter, Kristen, and her husband, Mark, are expecting their first little one in just a few months. What an exciting year this will be for us!

Babies and toddlers can be such a treat to care for, and there are so many cute things to make for them that I hardly know where to start. Of course, our principal concern is their health and well-being. We also want to make good use of our time, energies, and money. I hope the ideas I have to share with you will help you provide the best of everything for your own child or grandchild.

A good place to begin is with the food we feed our little ones. Be sure and check with your baby's doctor as to when he is ready for solid foods and about the kinds and variety of food a baby needs. Then you can really help your child by feeding him healthy foods that you prepare yourself. True, it may not be as easy as scooping it out of a baby food can or jar, but it really doesn't take that much work and your baby will certainly be better off.

Baby foods can be made at home from poultry, fish, meats, fruits and vegetables, prepared without seasonings, salt, and spices. Be sure that you remove all bone, fat, gristle, and skin when preparing meats. All fruits and vegetables should be well scrubbed and cooked (or steamed) in a very small amount of water.

After these things are cooked, your blender does the next step. A normal blender works fine, or you can purchase a little machine just made to blend baby foods. Serve the food at once and freeze what is left over (but use it within a month or so). I lined my styrofoam egg cartons with foil or plastic wrap to divide the food into baby-sized portions. Then I froze these little portions of smooshed-fruits or vegetables in a plastic bag for storage. If food is stored in foil, you can heat it up right in the foil.

Again, check with your doctor, but usually good fruits to start are applesauce, mashed bananas, peaches, or pears. Then a little later (at five to ten months) you can add apricots, pineapple, plums or prunes. I wouldn't recommend any kind of berries because they have seeds. Be sure your fruits are well ripened. For example, bananas should be yellow, flecked with brown.

To fix fruit for a baby, just peel and prepare as usual — cut the fruit up in pieces and steam it until it's nice and tender. Then blend it in the blender until it's smooth. Fresh fruit juices can also be made for your baby. And don't forget that your baby needs *water* too! Never, never, never put sweetened drinks and punches in your baby's bottle. They have little food value and aren't doing a bit of good for your baby but developing a taste for sugar.

Vegetables should be prepared the same way as fruits. The best ones to start a young baby on are beets, carrots, peas, and then sweet potatoes, and green beans.

Your doctor probably will also recommend starting your baby on egg yolk. When he does this, the best way I found to prepare it was to soft boil the egg (about three minutes) and stir the egg yolk into cereal. It's much more palatable this way.

The easiest way to prepare beef for baby food is to take a nice piece of frozen beef (never ground beef) and scrape it with an ordinary table knife. Put the smooth scrapings into a custard cup and cover it with milk, formula, or water, and set into a pan of simmering water. Have the level of the simmering water only about half way up the custard cup so that water won't splash into the food. Cover your pan with a lid and cook very slowly for about thirty minutes. Then it is ready to use or freeze.

As your babies become a little older, you will be able to puree about anything for them that you cook for a family meal. Just remember to add salt and other seasonings *after* their portion has come out. Soon you'll be able to just mash the food with a fork, and it won't be long before they will be eating a balanced meal right along with the rest of you. You'll save so much money and all feel better, too.

It won't be long—at around two years of age—before your youngsters will become a little picky and lose their appetites a bit. This is normal because their growth rate slows down. Don't force them. It can be the worst thing you do. It will only upset both of you. Offer them only good, nourishing foods in an attractive way, and they will eat when they are hungry. A relaxed attitude on your part pays dividends in so many ways with your children.

A fun thing to do with a slow eater, or one that is ill, is to serve his meal in a muffin pan, arranging the food in the order in which will eat it. Have him eat his way up to the top corner cup where a little treat is waiting, such as a food treat or a little note promising a story. Be sure and make your toddlers some of those good Graham Crackers and He-Man Cookies in Chapter 6. They are so good and good *for* them.

Food should also be attractively served on a plate. This helps to stimulate the appetite even in an adult. Mashed potatoes can become a fluffy cloud; a broccoli spear, a tree; a carrot slice, the sun, or a hamburger patty, a wheel with celery-stick spokes. Make a little car from a hot dog on a bun; carrot slices form the wheels and olives the headlights. With a potato chip road, and a few celery trees, a lunch becomes exciting.

It also helps to get children into the planning of meals. As they make out menus, they learn to include something from each food group. They enjoy charts at this age, so why not make each child a chart listing the daily diet requirements— grains and cereals; meat, egg and beans; milk and cheese; and fruit and vegetables—and they can list what they eat each day to see if they eat what is required. A special dessert is always a favorite reward at the end of a "well-balanced" week.

Just remember, healthy kids are happy kids. Keep a positive attitude and you'll survive mealtime.

Becoming a new grandmother has me excited about the cute baby things to make, and I'd like to share a few patterns with you. As you know, I like to have an afghan to pick up and work on at my "frustration" times, and a baby size is ideal. I'm no pro at crocheting, so I enjoy the ripple pattern because it doesn't take any concentration. You make it either solid color or in a color pattern. Here are the basic directions to make a 36-by-54 inch afghan:

Row 1 — Chain 186, 1 sc in 2 ch from hook, 1 sc in each of next 6 ch, *3 sc in next ch, 1 sc in each on next 7 ch, skip 2 ch, 1 sc in each of next 7 ch, repeat from * to last 8 ch, 3 sc in next ch, 1 sc in each of next 7 ch, ch 1, turn.

Row 2 — Skip 1 sc, 1 sc in back loop of each of next 7 sc, *3 sc in back loop of next sc, 1 sc in back loop of each of next 7 sc, skip 2 sc, 1 sc in back loop of each of next 7 sc, repeat from * to last 9 sc, 3 sc in back loop of each of next 7 sc, leave last st unworked, ch 1, turn.

After you have finished your afghan, you are bound to have a little yarn left, so why not crochet a 2-by-14 inch strip and cover a wooden hanger for the new mother's gift? Just poke the hook of the hanger through the middle of the strip and whip the piece together across the bottom and ends with a large needle and some matching yarn.

Naturally we'll want to make some quilts, and again, baby quilts are a good size to start on. First buy four pieces of 1-by-3 inch lumber, two pieces seven feet long and two pieces nine feet long, and four C clamps from the hardware store. For a very small investment you now have your quilting frame. Use four kitchen chairs to brace corners on and clamp the boards together at the corners to form the size quilt you want. After your frame is set up, your bottom piece of fabric gets tacked on first, right side *down*. With thumb tacks, tack it to the center of each board stretching it uniformly across. Then finish tacking each side so that it is pulled evenly taut. (You'll need one and a half yards of fabric for the bottom, another one and a half yards for the top of a baby-sized quilt.) I use about eight to ten thumb tacks down a side. I then purchase a polyester batting size 81-x-96 inches, cut it down the middle, and each piece in half. This gives me two double battings for baby quilts, which is a nice, fluffy thickness. After your bottom fabric is on the frame, lay your batting on and stretch carefully to fit. Tack also in a few places on all sides. Next, lay down your top piece of fabric, again tacking it at the center of each board and then securing it all around. At this point, be sure that all three layers are taut. If this is your first quilt, it really helps to have either a checked fabric or a design that is repeated every three or four inches. This gives you a guideline for stitching (stitches should never be more than three to four inches apart).

Next choose a matching (or contrasting) *washable* yarn, four-ply preferably, and a large-eye needle. Using a single strand of yarn, take a stitch every three or four inches through all thicknesses of quilt. Continue stitching a row along the quilt, leaving each loop of yarn between stitches very loose so that you have ample length to tie. When you have used up your needle full of yarn, go back and cut between stitches and tie ends into a secure square knot, then trim ends uniformly.

After you have worked as far into your quilt as you can reach, unscrew the C clamps on one end and roll the board under until you reach the point where you need to start quilting again. Again pull the board tight and secure both C clamps.

44 Repeat this process until the quilt is completed.

After it is all tied, you are ready to finish the outer edge. This can be done in several ways. I usually like an eyelet or self-fabric ruffle. Before edging, lay your quilt out on the floor and trim all sides evenly. Then pin or baste the ruffle, trimmed edge together, to quilt edge on the right side of quilt top. Sew it in place on the machine, then turn the quilt, press seam toward quilt and blind stitch the back to the quilt top covering the machine stitching.

You can also bind it with self fabric. For a half-inch finished binding, cut strips one and one-half inches wide. This will give you a one-fourth inch seam allowance on each edge of binding. Join all your strips together in one long, continuous strip of fabric. With right sides together, pin the binding on the quilt top. Stitch one-fourth inch from edge on the machine, then turn under one-fourth inch seam allowance on the other edge of binding and fold over to wrong side of the quilt. Blind stitch in place over machine stitching.

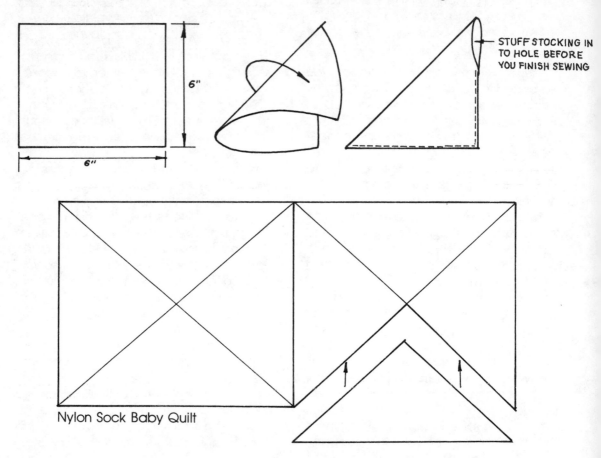

6"

6"

STUFF STOCKING IN TO HOLE BEFORE YOU FINISH SEWING

Nylon Sock Baby Quilt

A little lady in Roosevelt, Utah, taught me how to make a diamond edge. This is so pretty for a baby quilt and also really easy. It requires one yard of forty-five-inch wide fabric cut into four-inch squares. Fold the squares in half diagonally, then fold again to form a triangle. With right sides together, pin each triangle to edge of quilt (cut edges together) all around the quilt, overlapping triangles one inch. Sew in place on a sewing machine. Press triangles up with seam toward quilt. Turn quilt over and blind stitch the back to quilt top, covering machine stitching.

A super baby quilt can be made from nylon socks. We always have plenty of old nylons full of "runners" around. To make this quilt, just cut six-inch squares of fabric, fold each into a triangle, right sides together, and stitch two sides, leaving a small opening. Turn the triangle right side out and stuff a clean old nylon (toe and all, or if using pantyhose, cut each leg off and use the whole leg) into the triangle. I use a pencil to work it in evenly. Stitch up the opening (I do this on the machine). Then put four of the finished triangles together to form a square. These can be stitched together with an overcast stitch by hand, or I just usually use the zigzag stitch on my machine. Continue putting squares together until you reach the desired size. These quilts are so warm yet lightweight, and they are a dream to launder since they dry so quickly. Start saving your nylons today!

45

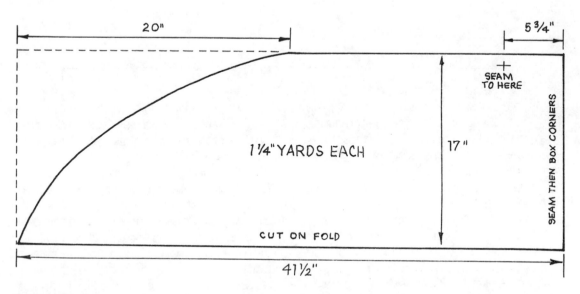

Bunting Pattern

18"

9"

My friend from Roosevelt also gave me this precious, yet easy, bunting pattern. They are so nice for babies because they are like a sleeping bag with Velcro fasteners, and babies won't come unwrapped like they do in quilts and blankets. In fact, I'm making my new grandchildren a bunting and *matching* quilt.

To make the bunting, cut your top and bottom fabrics and batting to fit the pattern piece. Then put the three layers on the kitchen table. Pin in several places to secure them together and then just tie as you would a quilt. (You don't need to use frames.) After it is tied, sew it up as directed on the pattern, and finish off the edges. They are so cute!

A favorite gift for young mothers and fathers are these little "burp" pads. Just cut two layers of terry cloth and edge with binding or ruffling. They fit perfectly over your shoulder, and look so much prettier than a diaper when you're in church or a public place. I like to embroider the word *Oops!* on the back or a little frilly trimming. These make a nice shower gift for pennies.

To make another unique shower gift, take a sardine can, well cleaned and free of sharp edges, paint the outside a pastel color and fill it with a scrap of tightly packed quilt batting. Cover a piece of white fabric to resemble a sheet, make a tiny quilt cover (maybe embroidered with the baby's name), add a ruffle around the edge, a tiny pillow, and you have a neat little bed-pin cushion. Sure comes in handy for those diaper pins!

triangle and cut in two along the fold. Place the point of the bandana triangle over the center of the washcloth and stitch the washcloth to the bandana. Hem the cut edge of the bandana and embroider (or use embroidery pens) "Hi, Pardner!" across the bottom of the washcloth. The two ends of the bandana are then tied around the little guy's neck and he's a regular cowboy.

While we are working with terry cloth,

I like to make bibs, too. The easiest and most practical are made from a fringe-edged fingertip towel. Just fold the top edge down toward the outside about three to four inches, cut a half circle in the center, and bind with bias tape, leaving strings for tying. Then you can decorate and trim them any way you like. They wash well and are absorbent. Mommies love them!

Our favorite bib is for that little boy. Purchase a white washcloth and a bandana. Fold the bandana in half like a

why not make an ideal "wrap up" towel for the little one? Babies can be pretty wiggly after a bath, and these towels work perfectly. A forty-five inch square is ideal, but a thirty-six inch one will work, too. Buy a square of terry cloth. Edge it with bias tape. If desired, a triangle can be sewn to one corner to slip the baby's head into. Then, of course, be sure and embroider it for the "Little Drip." In appliquing the "drip" on the towel, use a nylon taffeta or a light type of fabric that will dry quickly. You could even make a "Big Drip" towel for Dad. He'd love it!

little drip

You know, these dads take a lot of pride in that new baby. I love to hear my husband tell of his memories of rocking Stephen (our firstborn) in the middle of the night, and the thrill he felt as one night Stephen turned his little head up in recognition as Roy talked softly to him. He never fails to get a tear in his eye when he talks about the joy he felt then.

It's not long before the baby's big enough that we can start making playthings. The first and most useful thing to make is a quiet book. These are so fun to do because you can really use your imagination. They are made entirely out of fabric and are perfect for taking to church. Use a heavy-weight fabric like denim for the covers, and I like to use those big clip rings to put the pages together. Double each piece of fabric, forming one double

page with the fold as the outside edge of the page. In fact, you can use one long strip of fabric, folding it back and forth and back and forth to form the pages. It's simplest that way. Sew all your designs on before folding to form the pages. I am including several ideas for pages, and I'm sure you will think of many more. These are great to keep little fingers busy, and they are such a terrific learning tool.

I feel very strongly about the toys and playthings we provide our children. We too often take their creativity away. The flimsy plastic toys we spend so much money for today are soon broken and forgotten anyway. Why not provide long-lasting learning equipment? This "little town" map to be made of a heavy duck or canvas type fabric (just bind it with bias tape) can help your youngster learn about his town

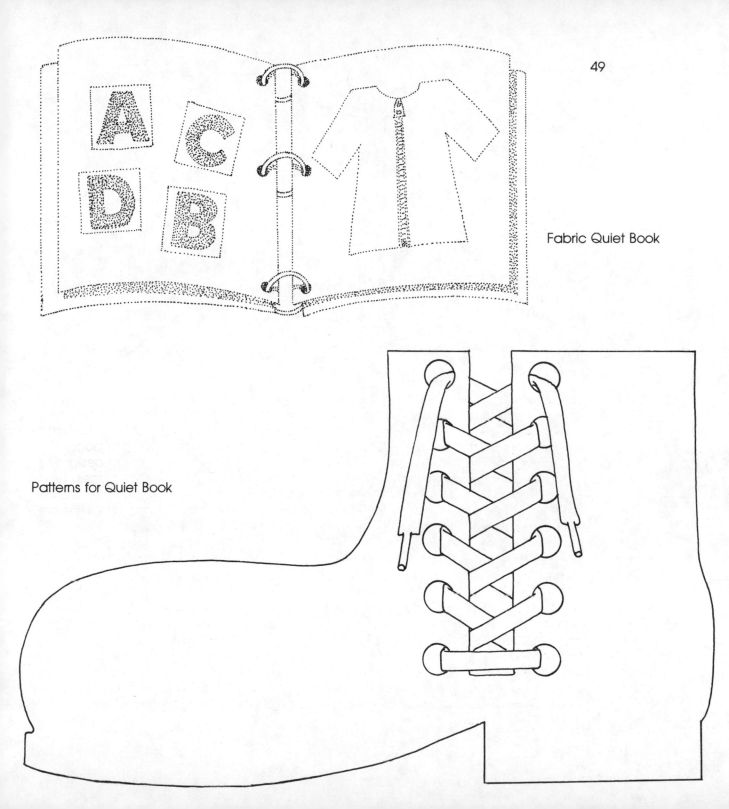

Fabric Quiet Book

Patterns for Quiet Book

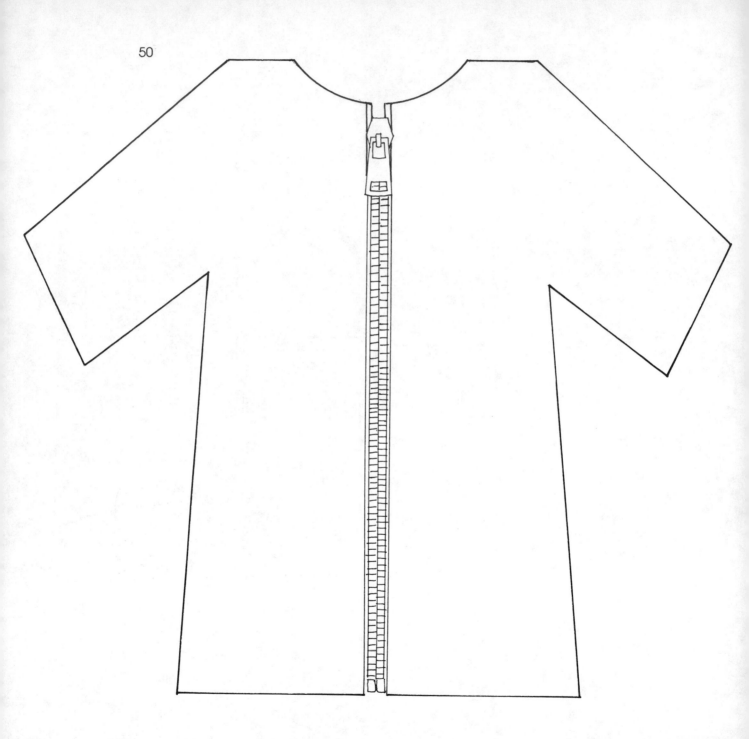

and create many hours of fun. This is just a simple pattern. Let him help you design the map of *your* area. Use permanent marking pens in different colors. He'll treasure this.

Everyone loves to create with his hands, and this "Sunshine Clay" will keep little fingers busy for a long time. In fact, the children help you knead the ingredients together and choose the colors to make it.

Sunshine clay will stay soft if you keep it in a plastic bag in the refrigerator and hardens if you leave it out. If your little girls would like to make beads, just form the beads from this clay, run a toothpick through them, dry on a cookie sheet in a 225-degree oven for about fifteen minutes on each side, and they're ready to be strung on shoelaces. Let them create beautiful jewelry!

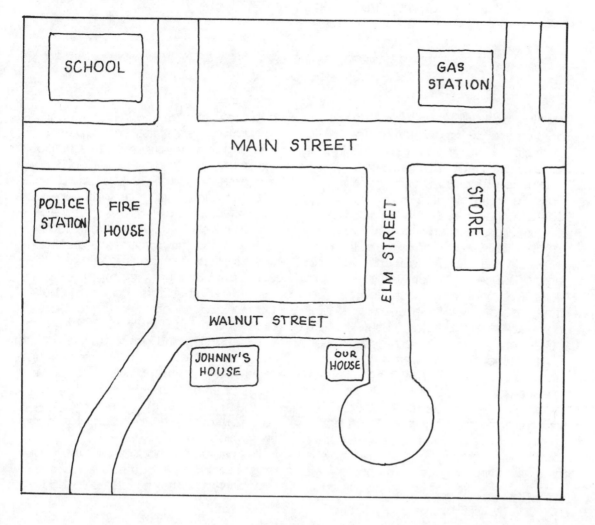

SUNSHINE CLAY

Knead together: 3 cups flour
1 cup water
1 cup salt
1/3 cup oil
Add: desired coloring

Our little girls also liked to make their own dolls. It's easy to fashion a rag doll, clothespin doll, or yarn doll, and in the summer don't let them miss the opportunity of a performance of "dancing" hollyhock dolls. It's worth planting a few just for this purpose. The flower, turned upside down, becomes a beautiful full, bell-shaped skirt, and the little green knob on the bottom will resemble the doll's head. They look so pretty, like real southern belles in hoop skirts. We spent many hours sitting on the front porch waltzing our beautiful hollyhock-skirted dolls around!

Why not let your little girls fashion their own dollhouse? It's worth a hundred commercial ones. Oatmeal boxes make great cradles; sardine cans (with no sharp edges!) neat tiny beds. Salt boxes, cut down, make super chairs; match boxes become tables or dresser drawers. Other boxes make furniture, and a plastic bowl is a terrific swimming pool. The house itself can be made from a few scraps of fabric and some glue and a big box—even they will be surprised at their masterpieces. Be sure and donate your empty thread spools for stools and end tables. Wool scraps make great wall-to-wall carpeting. Save your little lids and caps to be used as dishes (plates, bowls, glasses, flowerpots, wastebaskets, etc.) A few little feathers glued to a toothpick makes a cute broom. Scraps of yarn can be crocheted into little throw rugs. Small pocket mirrors become full wall length mirrors and a large button pasted on an empty thread spool makes a cute end table. Plastic tops from spray cans can become patio furniture. Things that are normally considered scraps and ready for the wastebasket can provide hours of entertainment. Remember how I suggested in *A Family Raised on Sunshine* to throw out your wastebasket and put everything to use?

I've never seen happier kids than those engaged in simple games like hopscotch, playing with a stick horse (fashioned from an old broom), handmade slingshots, carving soap or wood, or playing with a simple bean bag! You'll even have fun making these. A basket of frog bean bags is guaranteed to entertain any little guest that comes your way. It's even fun to draw a giant checker board outside and play "checkers" (or leap frog!) with these little frogs.

Have you given your children the opportunity to form their own band? No matter how little they are, it's surprising how much rhythm they can develop this way. A large oatmeal box becomes a drum. A plastic container with some beans in it is a great shaker. Two sticks good for beating a rhythm on an aluminum pie pan, or two wooden sticks, or a cymbal—you can

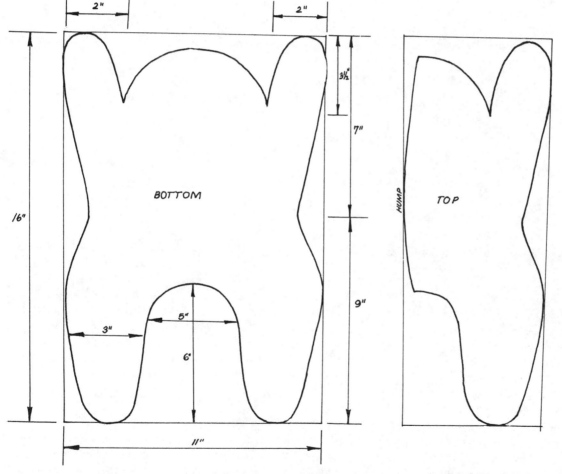

Frog Bean Bag

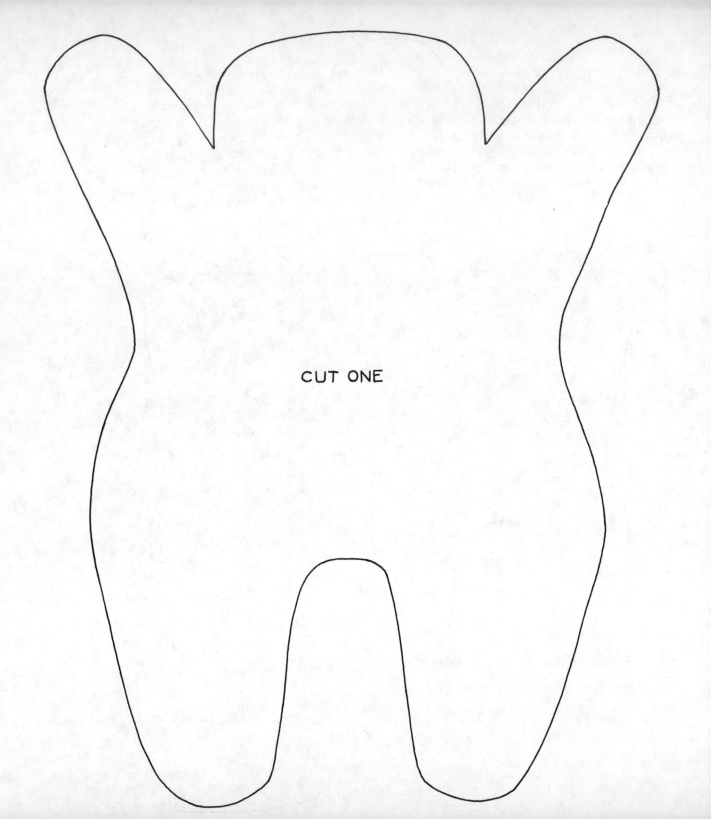

CUT ONE

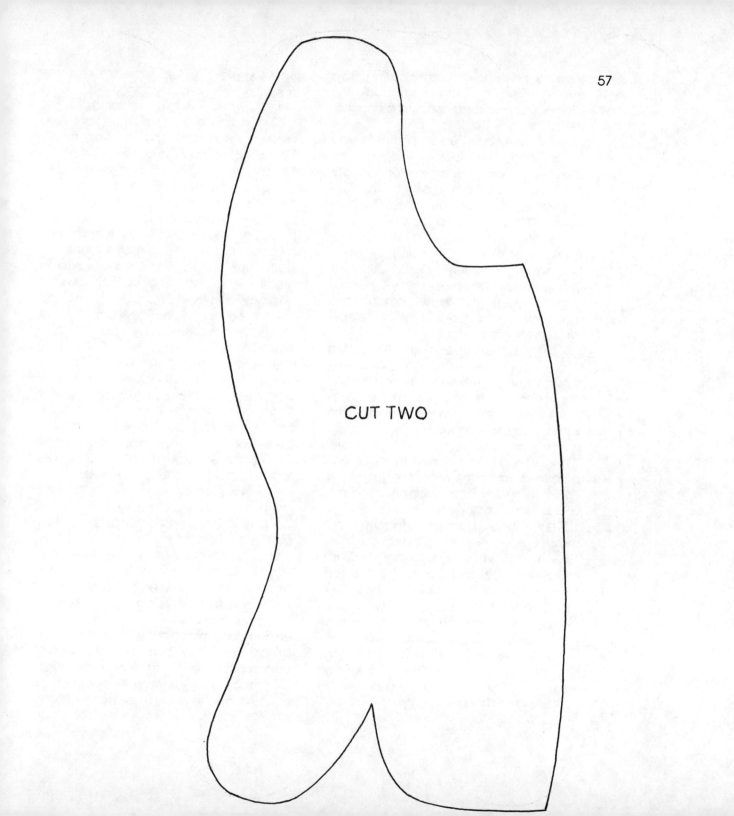

CUT TWO

even get one of the little ones puffing into a small-necked jug. They are so proud of the sounds they make. Try singing along with them. They will be so pleased!

If you have any budding artists at your house (and who doesn't, who has children!), just cut three large grocery bags open and tape them together with masking tape, forming one large sheet of paper. Have your child lay down on the paper and draw around him. Then he can spend the morning coloring himself — adding hair, features and clothing. If Grandma is many miles away, you may want to fold up the finished product and mail it to her in a big brown envelope. Wouldn't she be proud!

A fun way to entertain your preschoolers and have them learning at the same time is to cut out the letters of their name in stiff cardboard or thick polyfoam. You may want to cut felt to fit on top. Then hide the letters around the house showing your child on his fingers how many pieces there are. When he has found all the pieces, he can practice forming them together to spell his name. If you have more than one child, use a different color for each name.

Flannel boards are great teachers, but most of us leave them to the schools and churches. Cover a cardboard or foam square with felt, and then let the children cut out characters, clothes, and other things from felt to create their own stories. Every little scrap of felt can be used — even the tiny little pieces of blue can be raindrops and will keep those little fingers occupied for hours. Whenever I take my samples somewhere to give a presentation, I find a little one by my table totally occupied with the felt board. They love the way felt sticks to felt. It doesn't become frustrating like so many things do.

If you would like to make some little girl really happy, buy a small amount of a pretty quilted fabric (or use scraps), turn to Chapter 8, and cut the quilted fabric out in the gingerbread house pattern (be sure you also cut a bottom, though). Seam all the pieces together, leaving one side of the roof to lift up. Bind it with bias tape. This becomes the neatest little carrying box for all her little dolls and treasures. Once you start putting it together, you'll become creative — adding a door, windows, a chimney, and even appliquing a tree and flowers on one side. They can be just darling. A handle can even be added to the top.

Now don't forget the little boys. Few things make them happier than a few simple tools, chosen carefully to be safe for little hands. They will create a masterpiece! When our boys were both small, a couple of little hammers and a pile of rocks was all the entertainment they could ask for. My! the beautiful things they found inside those rocks; glittery diamonds, and jewels, as well as fascinating fossil designs. We had a few smashed fingers, but they always healed.

Specially picked wild flowers pressed in wax paper in the pages of a heavy book become decorations on birthday cards or stationery to friends; a jar of buttons becomes coins to play "store" with, a challenge to match colors, or something to string for jewelry. A bunch of cut strands of yarn can be drawn into a pretty picture on carpeting. My kids favorite pastimes as youngsters were a few small bowls of flour, corn meal, rice, sugar, water, food coloring, soda, salt, and baking powder. They had a great time mixing and stirring and making a mess, budding scientists around the kitchen table.

Little boys and girls are so precious. Thank goodness we have the privilege of being grandparents. It gives us the opportunity to catch up on a few of the joys we may have overlooked as parents.

Happy first day of your life, Emily Marie, from your new grandmother!

5

Over the River and Through the Woods

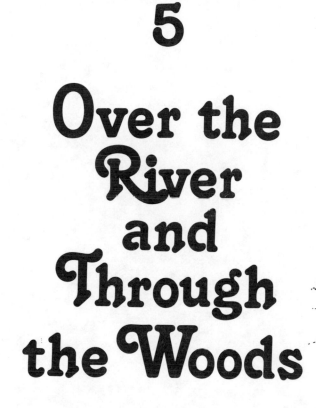

One of the choicest ways in which our family has built togetherness has been through picnics, camping, and vacations. Since Roy's employment has required that we move fairly often, we are fortunate to have favorite picnic spots all over the country.

In Olympia, Washington, we loved to drive to Priest's Point Park. I don't believe I have ever seen such straight, tall trees as we saw there. I am sure little Stephen, as he looked up from his stroller, felt overwhelmed by their size, but, my, how excited he was to feed the peacocks. They would strut by so cautiously, snatching the bread crumbs Stephen threw for them. Even peacocks seem to prefer whole-wheat bread. They always eat that first. It has always been interesting to me that most animals and birds choose their diets so well, yet man has not mastered that himself; see Chapter 6.

Our little picnics and trips in Washington were never complete without a stop at one of the beautiful fields of tulips and daffodils. The sight of several square miles full of colorful blooms really took our breath away. While we lived there, I picked up some little pointers about growing these flowers. Bulb growers consider it a must to plant tulips and daffodils in clusters, never in straight rows, and absolutely never in a single row.

If you have never force-grown some bulbs in early spring (Christmas to March) inside, you must try it. Here are the pointers the bulb growers gave me:

1. Use only plump, firm, healthy bulbs for forcing. Start with a shallow, leak-proof container, pebbles, and water.

2. Arrange a thin layer of peat moss, sand, or gravel on the bottom of the container.
3. Set your bulbs in upright position in the container.
4. Fill in around the bulbs with pebbles allowing the tips of the bulbs to stick out.
5. Sprinkle several pieces of charcoal in around the bulbs to keep the water sweet.
6. Add water up to the middle of the bulbs. Keep watered and in a cool area.
7. Enjoy your blooms!

When your first indoor bulbs bloom, plan a little picnic party on a blanket spread on the family-room floor. For dessert, try a "window box" cake: Bake a chocolate cake in a bread loaf pan. When the cake is cooled and out of the pan, frost all sides with a light green frosting flavored with mint, or you may wish to frost it with chocolate frosting and use the tines of a fork to simulate the weaving of a basket. This forms your window box. To form the flowers, insert a wooden meat skewer into three large marshmallows. Then, using a decorating tip or canned decorator icing, squirt small rosettes all over the marshmallows. Soon you will have a very real-looking "hyacinth." To form the leaves, roll out a large green gumdrop in sugar, turning often. When it is very thin (one-eighth inch) cut oblong leaves. These are then placed up the sides of the "hyacinth." With three of these flowers across your cake you have a very impressive "window box" and a very delighted family. Be adventurous and try other types of flowers, too. My gumdrop roses in *A Family Raised on Sunshine* look pretty this way.

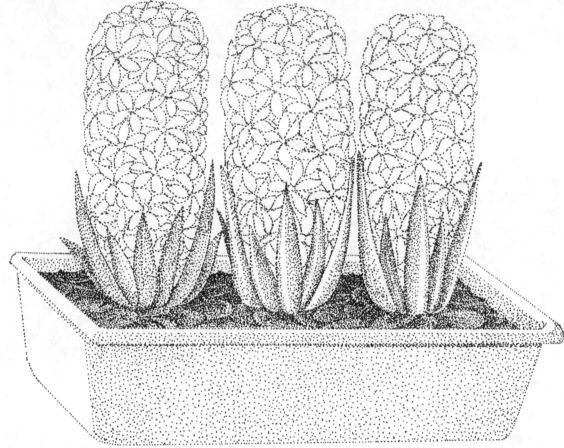

Another fun dessert is made by using new, well-scrubbed, three-inch clay flowerpots: Cover the bottom hole with foil and fill the pot one-third full of cake batter. Bake. When cakes are cooled (still in pots), put a scoop of ice cream on top and cover with meringue. Bake just a few minutes at 450 degrees until nicely browned. Pop a (real or fake) daisy on the top, and surprise! a baked alaska à la flower.

All of our picnics have not always been held in the summertime amid the blooming flowers. In fact, our most memorable picnic spot is located up Big Cottonwood Canyon out of Salt Lake City. Our family has always felt this little part of the world belonged to us. There has never been a time that we arrived for a picnic when it has not been waiting for us, unoccupied, peaceful, and inviting. Have you ever gone exploring, played with your little ones, and then had a delicious picnic of hot soup, relishes, and rolls, or hot dogs and a thermos of hot tomato soup, next to a mountain stream nearly frozen over with ice and surrounded by banks of snow

SNOW ICE CREAM

Beat: 2 eggs.
Add: 2 cups milk
    1 1/2 cups sugar
    1/2 tsp. salt
    3 tsp. vanilla

Mix: together well, and then just stir in clean snow until no more can be added. You can add fruits or any flavoring you desire.

SOURDOUGH STARTER

Dissolve: 1 pkg. dry yeast in 2 cups warm water.
Stir: in 2 cups flour.
Mix: this together in a glass or plastic bowl. (Never use metal.) Let stand, covered, on your counter overnight. (Don't refrigerate.) In the morning, remove 1/2 cup of the starter and store it in the refrigerator in a glass jar.

FOR PANCAKES
Add: 1 tsp. salt   3 T. oil
    1 tsp. soda 1 T. sugar
    2 beaten eggs to the remaining starter.
    Fry on griddle.

Next Time you want pancakes:
The night before, take out your 1/2 cup starter and
    Add: 2 cups milk
         2 cups flour
Let stand out overnight.
In the morning, remove 1/2 cup starter to store, and make pancakes as before.

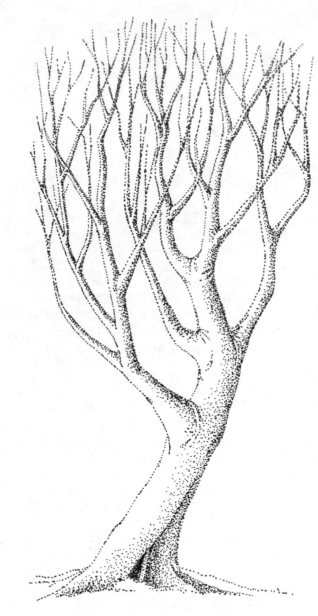

under huge pine trees? Try it! It is unforgettable!

Of course the boys' favorite thing to do was to have a good romp in the snow and then to have sourdough pancakes with ham and eggs in the morning.

They are fantastic! The flavor improves each time, and you never need yeast again. Why not share some starter with a neighbor, just like the pioneers?

Another big treat the kids always liked in the canyon in the winter was to make Snow Ice Cream.

Some people may worry about fallout or chemicals in the air, and I certainly wouldn't use the snow right in a city, but out in the country away from traffic or factories or up in the canyons, I think if you use nice clean snow, it surely doesn't have any more harmful things in it than many of the commercial foods we eat. (In fact, probably less.) Your kids will have so much fun, and so will you!

You don't have to have the mountains or a stream to have a fantastic winter picnic with the kids and your husband. There are so many places near our homes that lend themselves to a unique picnic spot for wintertime. Next time you have a good snow, bundle up and head for the nearest park. You will build memories your children will always treasure.

Roy has an appreciation for all of nature, and he has instilled this in the hearts of our family, who I know will carry it through their lives. On one of our winter picnics, we were struck with the difference and beauty of the trees without their leaves. We imagined each of them telling a unique story. Did his back become crooked because he forgot to stand straight while he was young? Or have the rains and snows he was called to bear been heavy? Were her branches bent by storms she was too weak to withstand? Did he grow straight and tall to the sun because of the encouragement from other straight ones around him? Was her bark scarred in a trial by fire? We have even had fun playing games with trees in the winter trying to think of a person the trees may have looked like or may have reminded us of. Try it! I guarantee you many laughs.

When we lived in Salt Lake City, another favorite picnic spot was Liberty Park, located in the heart of the city. Of course, kids loved to feed the ducks and animals, but it was here they learned an apprecia-

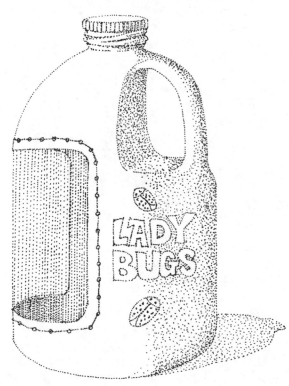

tion for history. Historical events came alive as the kids wore their pioneer outfits, and we had a picnic of Mormon cornbread and baked beans, envisioning the settling of the pioneers in the beautiful Salt Lake Valley.

Picnics by the Platte River are quite different from ones by a mountain stream in Utah but are exciting in their own way. In Nebraska, our favorite picnics were made up of delicious corn-on-the-cob (In Nebraska, what else? And, don't forget that teaspoon of honey in your water when you cook corn. But don't salt the water!) and some of their famous beef in our hamburgers. For a main dish, our kids loved to wrap a hamburger patty, a sliced potato (scrubbed well but not peeled!), a sliced carrot, onion, and celery in a sheet of foil. This is then placed in the coals and baked for about an hour. Delicious! If you are lucky enough to have some good roasting ears, wrap a strip of bacon around the ears in a swirl and wrap in foil and bake also. Boy! What a taste treat!

In Texas most of our picnics turned out to be hunts for lizards, rocks, and bugs (the joys of having sons), but there was always plenty of cold melon to refresh us. I think the best melons in the country come from Texas! By the way, when your kids are at the bug-collecting age, here are two fun projects for them to make. They are great to take along on outings and picnics.

The first one is a neat insect container, and I always liked it because I didn't have to worry about broken glass jars. Wash a plastic bleach bottle and cut a square from the side about 4-x-4 inches. Then punch holes along the edge of the square (don't make the holes too large). Take a piece of 6-x-6 inch nylon net and "sew" it over the opening with string going in and out of the punched holes. Hold the net in place with cellophane tape while stitching. Youngsters can spend hours with these. The names of the insects can be printed on the bottle with magic marker or the bottle can be decorated with colored flowers, etc.

All kids *have* to have a bug or butterfly net. Again, wash a bleach container well. Then draw a ring around the bottle about one and a half inches wide and cut it out. This will be used as the stable "hoop." Punch holes around one edge of the ring. Take a piece of 16-x-20 inch nylon net and fold it in half width-wise. Stitch across the bottom and up the sides of the tube of nylon. Then stitch it around the ring of plastic, weaving the string in and out of the punched holes. Then secure a dowel, stick, or reed (about twenty-four inches long) to the ring of plastic for a handle. The whole family will be fascinated with the beautiful butterflies you'll find. You could save and mount some in a frame as a reminder of the special picnic day. Just remember that some butterflies are scarce and should be let go to delight others and reproduce their kind.

Since we are now living in Cincinnati, our picnics are often related to historical events and antique hunting. This part of the country is so rich in history and tradition. One of the best things we can do for our children is to teach them to love and appreciate their heritage. How exciting it is for everyone to contemplate the Indians once roaming this part of the country, covered wagons winding their way up that hillside, or even pioneers trekking through the brush over there barefoot. Who knows, you may even be lucky and find an arrowhead or an interesting fossil. Our oldest son, Stephen, could really give us a history lesson with the fossils he would uncover. Too often we pass right over beautiful things of the world without even being aware that they are there. What could be more intriguing than signs of the past etched out in a hillside, riverbed, or tree trunk. Don't overlook the enjoyable learning experiences you have right in *your* backyard. With so many things to

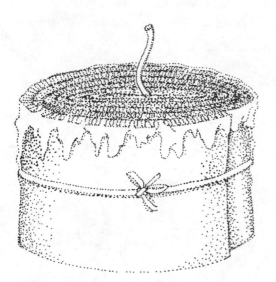

learn about in this great big wonderful world, how can anyone be bored? Just sitting on the porch studying the cloud patterns can be a unique experience.

Since we are a family of nature lovers, we especially love to go camping. There are two things I think you can never have enough of when picnicking or camping: washcloths and blankets. This is where I put my "waste not—want not" philosophy to work again. I save all of our worn-out bath towels and cut and hem them into nice-sized washcloths. I also save all old blue jeans, denim jackets, etc., and cut every available square of fabric from them, large or small. I then piece them together to form a quilt top. We have had some fun family evenings with everyone designing and decorating the squares with pictures or letters cut from iron-on tape. Plain fabric can be used for making the designs, using Stitch Witchery as bonding. Many pictures and items on these squares relate to former

outings we have had: that tree stump Heidi scraped her leg on (she still has a scar to prove it), those pretty flowers Kristen picked for our little centerpiece, the beautiful mountain trout Mark caught, Steve's favorite spinners and flys, the outhouse Kristen refused to enter, the tent with the crickets in it (Kristen didn't like that either; she's not fond of bugs!), the watermelon cooling in the stream, and our favorite bridge. Of course you could embroider or applique these things, but on an outdoor quilt, iron-on designs are much more practical.

After we cut out and iron the designs, we are ready to assemble the quilt. I use an old, worn blanket as a batting and put a patterned, dark-colored flannel as the backing. We usually tie the quilt with a dark matching yarn. Remember, never space your knots more than four inches apart. It is then easy to bind or hem the whole thing on your sewing machine. This type of quilt can be done spread out on the floor. However, quilting frames are so easy to make, so I prefer using them (see Chapter 4). The nice part about this type of quilt is that denim is one fabric that pine needles won't penetrate. So, not only do you use up old clothing, it is the best quilt you can have for camping and picnicking.

Two other items we feel are very helpful to our camping are our tuna-can burners and fire starters. These are fun to make as a family evening project and also use up materials we might have thrown away.

To make a tuna-can burner: Wash out an empty tuna can and cut strips of corrugated cardboard the height of your can. Roll the strips and fill the cans in a coiled fashion. After the can is tightly

packed we melt down our old candle ends (remember my love of candles?) or melt down some paraffin, pour melted wax over the cardboard, and insert a small wick in the center. They give a steady flame without being messy. They can be used for cooking alone for that one pan of stew. Just place several large rocks touching together to form a circle, set the burner down inside the circle, and set your pan of stew (or frying pan of eggs or pot of soup) over the burner resting on the circle of rocks. Or set a burner inside a larger can with an opening cut on the side and holes punched in the top for air.

Our other great helper is our simple fire starter. Since the boys and Roy enjoy woodwork and building, we always have plenty of sawdust around. We always save this sawdust and put it in the cups of cardboard egg cartons. Then, again, we pour melted candle ends in the cups of sawdust. After they are cool and hard, cut them apart, and boy! are they neat little

BEAN RELISH

Into large bowl combine:
> 1 one-pound can kidney beans
> 1 one-pound can French green beans
> 1 one-pound can yellow wax beans
> 1/2 cup chopped celery
> 1/2 cup chopped green pepper
> 1 chopped onion
> 1/2 cup salad oil
> 3/4 cup vinegar
> 2/3 cup sugar
> dash of salt

Mix: well together and refrigerate overnight. Keeps well and tastes better each day!

"THE BEST" POTATO SALAD

Boil: 12 medium potatoes in their skins until tender (red potatoes are always best for potato salad — white potatoes get mealy). Hard boil 12 large eggs.

Chop the cooled potatoes and eggs into a bowl along with 1 large onion and 1 green pepper.
Stir in 1 quart Miracle Whip salad dressing, a good dash of salt, pepper, and cayenne! This is a must! Really makes it super. Taste for seasoning. Feeds 10 nicely.

PICNIC SQUARES

Beat together:
    3/4 cup salad oil
    2 cups packed brown sugar
Add: 4 eggs and mix well
Then add:
    2 1/3 cups whole wheat flour
    2 tsp. baking powder
    1/2 tsp. salt
Mix well and add:
    1 6-oz. package chocolate chips
    1 cup rolled oats
    1/2 cup raisins or currants

Spread in greased 10-x-15 inch jelly roll pan and bake for 25 minutes at 350 degrees.

fire starters! If you don't have any sawdust available just go to your local lumberyard and they will give you plenty.

On our campouts, the boys and Roy are usually busy hiking or fishing. The girls and I aren't too fond of real (or rubber) worms but we do get to enjoy the fringe benefit of fresh fish: My two favorite ways of preparing fish are so simple. To fry: Beat 2 eggs and 1/2 cup milk together. Dip fish in flour, then into milk mixture, then coat with corn meal and fry in hot fat. Serve with fresh lemon wedges.

To poach (this is delicious, try it!): Put fish into cold frying pan, cover almost completely with cold water. Add one small carrot, small onion, celery stalk, salt and pepper to taste and one bay leaf. Cover, bring to a boil. Reduce heat and simmer about 10 to 15 minutes until fish is white and transparent and flakes easily. Don't overcook. Drain thoroughly and serve with fresh lemon squeezed over (or if you're trying this recipe at home, with hollandaise sauce and parsley).

On our outings our whole family loves to collect pine cones and other seed pods, weeds, and unusual things of nature. (By the way, pine cones dipped in melted wax are great fire starters too. I like to use these

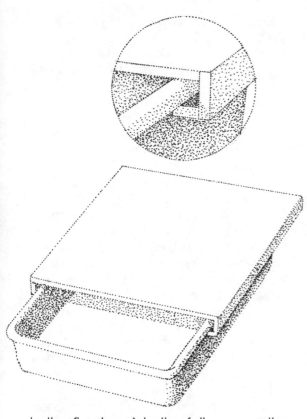

in the fireplace.) In the fall, we use the collections we have gathered to make nature wreaths. You'll find these are easy, pretty, and blend with any decor. They make nice Christmas gifts or gifts to take to a family on a Thanksgiving visit. In Chapter 8 you can find the instructions for making nature wreaths.

Naturally, camping and picnics are not complete without eating, and I must share with you three of our favorite picnic recipes.

Always make potato salad the day before and refrigerate it overnight so the flavors blend and mellow. Potato salad should never be served immediately after

making. Husbands will love this salad, I promise you! Always serve potato salad well chilled, and outdoors, remember to keep it on ice.

With our parents and families scattered around the county, we have many long trips, and with four small children this could be a problem. However, we've had lots of fun turning traveling by car into a challenge and building happy memories.

When the kids were very small, the biggest treat was the chance to be the one to sit in the front seat with us. They still laugh and remember the trip in which I kept an alarm clock in the glove compartment. Whenever it rang, the next one got to sit in front. This idea saves many complaints and tears. For one trip, before we left, I went to the local novelty and craft supply and bought two dollars worth of tiny games, puzzles, etc. These were kept in the compartment and given as prizes as we played our games. Children love to watch for three white cars, a single red flower, etc.

Another vacation I got each child a small plastic dish pan. Roy built a little wooden top that slid on and off (just two strips of wood on the bottom of a small piece of paneling). In it they each had things they enjoyed doing: crayons, books, etc. In Kristen's, I put a tiny, inexpensive doll (she later became "Lulu") and made a bunch of very simple clothes. Kristen was so delighted that she spent her entire trip playing with her. Whenever we stopped, she was watching for a pretty little flower, rock, leaf, or some accessory for Lulu. That year they all used their container to collect the souvenirs they got along the way. It was a fun and "organized" trip for all of us.

I am sure many passing motorists have

wondered about us as we have traveled across country, but we love to sing. Sometimes the car nearly rocked as we would get going on "You Are My Sunshine" or "She'll be Coming Around the Mountain." It has been a good time for us to learn the kids' favorite songs and for us to teach them some oldies like "Mairzy Doats." We even get some pretty good harmony sometimes, and Kristen's ukelele or Dad's whistling adds some interesting notes. A fun way to start singing while you travel is to flip the radio on just long enough to hear one note and pitch and then start singing the first song that comes to mind. Keep score to see who thinks of the most songs.

The latest game Mark made up for our family is to take three consecutive letters from the license plate in front of us and be the first to think of a word using those letters in that order. It's a challenge. He or Kristen (who are English and business majors) usually win. We don't hold a candle to them!

Speaking of license plates, our favorite game is played on *every* trip we take. Each person is given a map of the United States, and as we each see a license from a particular state, we are allowed to color in that state on our map. We get involved in our game for hours, and we've all learned a lot about our country's geography. There is always a grand prize for the winner of the game when we return home—a book about our country is a great prize.

Some friends of ours, the Smarts in Chattanooga, Tennessee, shared a game with us called "graveyard" that's really fun. First, organize teams on each side of the car; then, decide what kind of animal you are going to watch for, such as cow, horse, etc., each team only counting on their side of the car. You decide on a winning number before you start, and the first team to reach that number in their counting wins. If you come to a graveyard on your side you a have to bury all your cows and start over. It's good for lots of laughs.

Togetherness and closeness can be a happy reality if traveling is approached with a positive attitude. We put this to the test literally when all six of us (all adults—and the boys are six-footers) climbed into our little Toyota and took a trip to Niagara Falls and through Canada. Can you believe, not one cross word the whole trip? We had many laughs, though, as we piled out at service stations like clowns at a circus. The attendant usually just stood and shook his head. We loved it!

I really hope you are looking forward to the next outing with your family. A few dollars saved for a special little trip will give them cherished memories. I promise you it will mean more to them ten years from now than that new lamp you have been wanting for the living room. Remember, with our families, it's the doing and not the having—that's what families are all about.

6
A
Handful
of
Green
Thumbs

I hope you and your family are taking time to enjoy nature and all that the seasons have to offer. There is so much to learn and appreciate and the therapeutic benefits are priceless. I love that little saying, "Take time to smell the flowers." How many simple beauties of life we miss as we go through our hurried days.

Spring really seems like the time in which all life begins. Isn't it fun to see the first buds popping out on the trees, the yellow of the willows as you drive through the country-side, or the little shoots coming up from the moist fresh soil? Roy's favorite signs of spring are the sounds of the birds. He knows all the songs, and he and Steve could watch and listen to them for hours. It's one of the reasons he enjoys working in the yard so much. As they sing, he answers them with their call, and by golly, they seem to be carrying on a regular "conversation"! He always leaves some scraps of twine, thread, string, etc. out around the trees in the spring so he can watch the birds gather items to build their nests.

Of course, every yard should have a bird bath in the spring. You can get all kinds costing from ten dollars up to hundreds of dollars; but the birds use the cheaper ones just as much. You can even make one from an old garbage can lid, hub cap, pan or dish of some sort. Just be sure you make them look attractive – both the birds and your neighbors will appreciate that. If you use a shiny metal be sure you cover the bottom with rocks. Otherwise the birds could get burned in the hot sun. We have ours right out by the bay window so we can enjoy watching them while we eat. It is interesting how each variety of bird has its own unique way of bathing. Grackles are

by far the messiest. And robins must be the cleanest. They seem to enjoy it most and come most often. Robins come in large numbers, but for some reason they only go in the water one at a time. Keep the bird bath clean and rinsed out with fresh water. Birds are particular, too. It's also a good idea to have it fairly close to shelter for them if they get startled, but not too close to trees or shrubbery that could hide predators such as cats. Put a bird bath in your yard, and you'll have many hours of enjoyment.

Spring is such an exciting time. Things are changing fast, and new wonders of nature unfold each day, but don't get too rushed. Take time to look, smell, and feel the changes going on around you. It's good for the soul, and it will make you realize how blessed you are.

There is lots to be done in the spring, and our family can hardly wait to rake the yard and plant the garden. It makes me think of a quote by Jerrald, "If you tickle the earth with a hoe, she laughs with a harvest."

From the time the kids were tiny, they each had a little plot to care for. They were so excited as we planned and discussed what seeds to plant and the proper care of each. I think I'll remember forever how diligently little Kristen worked in her special rock garden. She treasured those pretty lillies of the valley and was so proud as she'd put them in little vases around the house. Not one weed ever crowded their growth, and she loved every little plant.

The boys were always planning how they could get the highest yield and possibly earn a few dollars. They got to be pretty shrewd in their planting.

Heidi always wanted to plant whatever

grew the fastest, and I remember one year she had lettuce coming out her ears. It's a good thing she loves salad!

In addition to our garden, when we lived in Kansas City the kids had their pet cemetery under the pine trees next to the garden plot. This always had to be tended in the spring with fresh flowers and new rock markers placed around. The year we buried Hans, our dachshund, out there was a sad time, and he had a very special marker and flowers on his grave all summer.

Even though we have moved a lot, we have always tried to have our yards be productive. We plant shrubs or bushes that will produce berries. If there is a space, we always try to add a few fruit trees. It's amazing how much fruit you can get from a dwarf tree, and if you get good stock, many varieties bear the second year. Be sure you check with your nurseryman, though. With some trees, you must have two together for pollination. It's also a good idea to check with him for spraying and pruning schedules, etc. There's nothing quite like picking big, plump, juicy peaches or apples off your own tree. The dwarf trees grow easily and really don't require much care. We sprinkle moth flakes around the trunk of the trees and work it into the soil a little to help keep away borers.

Another must for every yard in the spring is an outdoor clothesline. It's the best remedy for the "blahs" I can think of. I love to go out on a fresh spring morning and hang my sheets on the line. I know it takes me longer than it should but the smell of the air and all the magic sounds keep me spellbound, and I hate to go back into the house. After the sheets have basked in the sun and fresh air all day, I make up the beds again. And let me tell you, you don't need any pills to help you fall asleep. There's nothing quite like those fresh sheets. If you don't have an outside clothesline, I recommend it to everyone. It's cheaper than tranquilizers and lots more effective.

There's no better way to get acquainted with your neighbor than across the clothesline. Much counsel, advice and "cheering up" have come this way. Clotheslines even pay off in the wintertime. If you hang your white things, sheets, towels, etc. out and they freeze "stiff," it serves as an excellent bleach. Try it sometime! I remember many happy times shared with my Mom on the farm in Nebraska as we hung sheets out and then brought them in in the afternoon as stiff as a board to let them dry in the kitchen. What a fresh, crisp, clean smell, combined with the kettle of bean soup simmering on the old "cook stove." That was *Monday* to me.

Now let's get on to our garden plots. Be sure you pick a spot that gets *at least* six hours of sunshine every day. If you don't have room for a big garden, remember to make every spot in your yard count. Things like lettuce, peppers, even cabbage plants can serve as a border along a drive or walk. A little tub on your patio can be a great planter for a tomato plant, and it's a great way to grow a few yams. Just cut an *untreated* yam in two or three pieces so you have an "eye" or two on each piece, and plant them in a container. A bushel basket, tub, small garbage can, bucket or wooden barrels all work great. Just be sure to put drainage holes in the bottom. When the sprouts are about six to eight inches high, surround them with a mulch of peat moss or straw. This way they develop more roots and produce more yams. The greenery is really pretty, and when it dies down, you'll have a nice cluster of yams down in the soil. (By the way, yams are dark orange and moist where sweet potatoes are more yellow and on the dry side. Some people say that there is no difference, but there sure is!)

Plan your garden space well so that early plants are started indoors (besides, that helps you get the gardening "bug" a little earlier and really puts you in the mood). It's fun to start your own plants from seed. It's also easy and lots less expensive. Just plant your seed in some good "starting" soil (equal parts of potting soil, sand, and vermiculite) in egg cartons or plastic trays. Keep an old "squirt bottle" handy to keep the soil moist. After the seedlings have two sets of leaves, set them in direct sunlight and thin them so that you will have good strong plants ready to set out at the proper time.

You'll have more starts than you can use, so at Eastertime take some of your little seedlings and put them into your colored eggshell halves when you eat the Easter eggs. (Just cut your boiled eggs in half with a knife and scoop out the egg half.) They make a nice little gift to give a neighbor or friend and can be set right into the ground in the eggshell.

It's a good idea to have a little cold frame outside, and these are easy to make. A *cold frame* is a kind of hothouse, which can be as simple as a flat wooden box set into the ground and covered with a sheet of glass. To make a cold frame, outline the space with four boards. You can use anything from a door frame to a small orange crate, depending on the size you need. Railroad ties, though not always inexpensive these days, are treated to prevent rotting. You can also use cinderblocks or old bricks. Fill in the cavity with good, rich soil, then lay a piece of glass over the top to form a type of hothouse. Then when your little plants are ready you can put them out in the cold frame for a few days before they go into the ground. The transition won't shock them this way. A cold frame is also handy to start seeds of plants that have to be set into the ground later in the season. Try using an old shoe horn to transplant the little seedlings. It works great!

Planting our garden becomes a family joke because Roy uses a string and marker and always has nice straight rows. I just draw a line and drop in the seeds as I go, so some of my rows are a little crooked. My beans taste just as good as his, but he doesn't think so! I always like to plant a row of onions all the way around the garden, because I believe a rabbit won't cross over a row of onions. My family laughs at me about this, but I always have my row of onions anyway (and it gives me a crop from a space that would otherwise be wasted).

We always like to plant plenty of beets because we love fresh young beet greens cooked and served with butter, salt, pepper, and a touch of garlic. They are so tender and out of this world. Beets have to be thinned anyway, so this way nothing goes to waste. We all enjoy cooked beets as a vegetable, and then I like to be able to can lots of pickled beets (see *A Family Raised On Sunshine*). Remember to keep the dirt mounded up on your beets as they get bigger. If much of the top protrudes out of the ground, the beet will become woody. Don't let them get too big—three to four inches is enough.

We also like spinach cooked, so we plant plenty of that, but I enjoy it most used fresh in a salad. The best meal there is in the spring is a fresh salad made from the tender new leaves of spinach and lettuce, radishes and green onions, a wedge of cheese, and a slice of hot bread out of the oven. That is food fit for a king. Spinach grows best in cool weather, so plant in early spring or late summer. Sprinkle the plants with vegetable dust to help keep away insects.

So many people think of radishes as merely something to slice into a salad or to nibble on with a meal, but there is lots of good nutrition in them. A delicious treat we all enjoy is a radish sandwich. Just spread some fresh homemade bread with butter, slice a few radishes on it, sprinkle with a little salt, and enjoy with a cold glass of milk. That beats a gourmet dinner, any day. We always have the best luck in our garden with while icicle radishes and they are our favorite kind (white radishes are usually hotter than red). Be sure and thin your radishes when they are about two inches tall, leaving the strongest-looking sprouts and allowing one to two inches between each one.

Heidi's favorites in the garden are green peas and string beans. When she picks peas, she eats more fresh from the pod than she gets picked, but that's the fun of a garden. With both of these vegetables, remember the more you pick, the bigger the crop you'll get, so keep them picked every few days.

With peas, plan to plant two crops; one in spring and one in midsummer for a fall crop. They need fertile soil and lots of sun. As soon as the vines stop bearing, pull them up and plant a summer vegetable in the space (such as brussel sprouts or broccoli).

When your beans are several inches high, thin to about four inches between plants. Keep them well cultivated so they develop a good root system. We've had lots of fun conversations while we've sat together snapping beans. That's just one of the extra benefits you get.

Now if you grow some peas, you must have a hill or two of potatoes. Nothing can compare to fresh peas and newly dug, tiny potatoes in cream sauce. I cook my peas and potatoes separately, make a white sauce of one tablespoon flour to one tablespoon margarine cooked together, and add one cup milk. Stir until thickened, add salt and pepper to taste, then add the peas and potatoes and put a glob of butter on top with a little sprinkle of fresh parsley. That is so delicious. Spring isn't complete without it.

There are lots of types of squashes available. Our favorites are zucchini for summer and butternut for fall. Try chopping a fresh, raw zucchini up in your salad. It's delicious. It gives that same chewy texture as fresh mushrooms, and it's lots cheaper. So many of the vegetables we normally eat cooked are really better raw (and better for us). Try cutting up a bunch of zucchini, carrots, celery, radishes, turnips, rutabagas, broccoli, and cucumbers into strips and serving them on a warm evening with this tremendous dip. A few crackers to

McCROBY'S YUMMY VEGETABLE DIP

Combine: 1 1/2 cups sour cream
    2 1/2 cups mayonnaise (not salad dressing)
    1 cup finely chopped onion
    1 cup finely chopped green pepper
    1/2 cup finely chopped canned pimiento
    2 tsp. salt
    1/2 tsp. pepper
    Dash of tabasco
    1/4 tsp. garlic powder

Chill thoroughly before serving.

along with this, and your family or guests will lick the platter clean.

We also like to make lots of pickles, so cucumbers are a must. We grow them up on trellises so they don't take up so much space and are easier to pick. Cucumbers are like beans and peas. The more you pick, the more you get; and since we like our pickles small, I check the vines every day or two. It's no trouble at all to make a jar or two of simple garlic dills, and soon I have a nice shelf full. (For recipe see *A Family Raised on Sunshine*.) Be sure and make your pickles as soon as possible after picking so they'll be nice and crisp. I like to pick mine in the cool morning while they are still fresh with the dew.

Every garden must have tomatoes, and remember to fertilize them when the fruits start to form. You'll be guaranteed a bumper crop. Oh, how we love fresh tomatoes from the garden, again with a wedge of cheese and some homemade whole wheat bread. Isn't it fun eating in the summer, and we all feel so much better. Good, fresh fruits and vegetables and exercise in the garden can't hurt anyone.

We save so much money with a garden—not only through the food, which is a big item, but also in recreation. We don't have to drive somewhere else to do something. Working together in the yard brings a closeness that nothing else can bring.

The highlight of our garden is our rhubarb patch. On many a spring day my husband or one of the boys heads for the patch with a salt shaker. They just pull a stalk, cut off the top, then sprinkle with salt, and yum, is it good! Kinda makes your mouth pucker, like eating a green apple. I love it stewed for breakfast with whole wheat toast. I dice rhubarb and freeze it in bags, and cook up a bunch into sauce and can it. That way, if I'm in a hurry, I can open a jar for breakfast or as a treat. It's so handy to have. Just remember that rhubarb leaves are poisonous, so don't use them. Also always grasp the stalks and *pull* them out — never cut them off. This promotes more growth. I am amazed at the number of people who have never tasted rhubarb. If you are one of them, give your taste buds a real treat. Hot rhubarb pie has to be "the living end"! Be sure and try this delicious dessert, too!

Next to our vegetable garden, I think I love our herb patch best. In Colonial days, it was a "must" to have an herb garden outside the kitchen door. I can certainly

LAZY ROSY RHUBARB

Melt: one stick margarine
in casserole dish.
Combine: 1 cup flour
1 cup sugar
1 T. baking powder
2/3 cup milk

Pour evenly over melted margarine but do not stir. Add 2 1/2 cups of rhubarb sauce. Pour evenly over batter, but do not stir. Bake at 350 degrees for 1 hour or until nicely browned. Serve with ice cream or half and half.
To make rhubarb sauce:
Put 3 cups diced rhubarb into saucepan.
Add: 1/4 cup water.
Bring to a boil. Reduce heat and simmer until tender — about 10 minutes. Stir in 1/2 cups sugar and cook for a minute or two longer.

see why. The fragrance alone is worth it. There are several herbs that I think are a must. The first, of course, is parsley. Parsley seeds have a hard coating and need to be soaked in warm water overnight to help them germinate; then start them in little pots to be ready to set out when the weather is warm. Parsley is such a hardy growing plant and it can be used every day on the table. It adds prettiness to a dish as well as good flavor. And a sprig of parsley makes a great natural breath freshener. I also have chives (just buy a clump at the grocery store, set it in a dish of water until the roots are ready and set it outside) snipped up in salads or casseroles. It gives a very light onion flavor. It's pretty, too.

Then there's sweet basil and oregano. These are both easy to grow and what pizza, spaghetti sauce, or meat loaf is complete without them? Basil repels mosquitoes so it's extra nice to have around.

We also have mint. It grows like the dickens, but it's so fun to have. I always have some planted by the back door, and everyone going in or out grabs a leaf to chew on or at least rub between their fingers for the scent.

You should plant a little sage, too. After all, it's supposed to make us wise! It is so good in any chicken dish.

Dill is very important. Where would my cucumbers be without some nice fresh dill? It grows two to four feet tall and will reseed itself, so put it to the back of the herb garden.

The one herb I plant strictly for its scent is lavender. Why not! Ooh, it smells so good and has so many uses, be sure you try this one.

Since Colonial times, efficient gardeners have planted their herb gardens in patches or clumps rather than rows. It's fun to use an old wagon wheel and fill each variety in between the spokes. You can also divide off little sections of your area with railroad ties or even just slate or bricks. Some of these herbs are spreaders, though, especially mint, so be sure to confine them in some way.

Be sure you have some garlic and onion planted—not only for cooking, but also as a handy natural insecticide for your garden. Just put a chopped onion or a clove of garlic (or both) in a jar of water and let it stand a few days. Then spray the water on outdoor plants to repel bugs.

Now that you have everything planted and doing well, it's time to enjoy the summer. Be sure and keep your garden mulched with old straw or grass clippings. It saves lots of weeding time and watering. If one area of your garden doesn't get as much sun as the rest, you might lay strips of aluminum foil down instead of mulch. It serves the same purpose and will also repel some bugs and reflect light to help your growth and yield. Also, while the evenings are still a little cool, and you have a fire in the fireplace to take the chill off, be sure and save your wood ashes. They are great to sift over plants to help keep the bugs down, too.

Summer days are the times to relax on the patio with a good book or just enjoy the fluffy clouds blowing by. Most of the hard work is done, and we can begin to enjoy the harvest. I don't think there is a prettier picture than a basket of freshly picked vegetables.

Summer evenings are the times we can

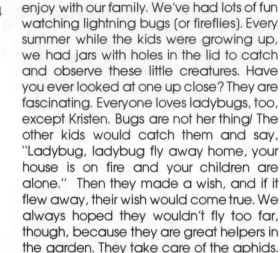

enjoy with our family. We've had lots of fun watching lightning bugs (or fireflies). Every summer while the kids were growing up, we had jars with holes in the lid to catch and observe these little creatures. Have you ever looked at one up close? They are fascinating. Everyone loves ladybugs, too, except Kristen. Bugs are not her thing! The other kids would catch them and say, "Ladybug, ladybug fly away home, your house is on fire and your children are alone." Then they made a wish, and if it flew away, their wish would come true. We always hoped they wouldn't fly too far, though, because they are great helpers in the garden. They take care of the aphids.

Be sure as the summer days pass by that you don't forget to have the kids go out and scrape their names on a pumpkin. As it grows and matures, the writing swells. It's so fun to watch. This can also be done on other hard-shelled things like gourds or winter squash.

The hot lazy days of summer go fast, but the exciting fall days begin. Harvesting all the crops and picking apples while that crisp air blows in my face, I get a real spurt of energy. I guess it's the pioneer spirit in me, but I love canning, freezing, and drying my harvest, and feeling that my larder is full and I am prepared. I always think of the scripture that says, "...if ye are prepared ye shall not fear" (Doctrine and Covenants 38:30), and the Parable of the Ten Virgins. I know that if I do my part, the Lord will bless my family.

As I gather in all the nice potatoes, it reminds me of a taste treat you must try. Remember, don't ever peel away those vitamins if you don't have to. But, if you *have* to peel your potatoes, go ahead and scrub them well first, and then save the peelings. For a real treat, french fry the *peels* in hot oil. They are absolutely delicious. You'll never throw another one away. They are so good for you, and I understand they are a real delicacy in France.

For the sake of space, I dry a lot of my fruits and vegetables (see method in *A Family Raised on Sunshine*). In addition to all the beans, carrots, onions, green peppers, etc. that I dry, I can save the small pieces to dry for soup mix or to bake into a vegetable bread or muffin. Just spread out all the little pieces of chopped vegetables (after they've been blanched) onto a brown paper bag and let them sit in a sunny window until dry and crisp. I love to use these in baking, and they still contain nearly all their nutrients. Once you've gotten some experience drying your fruits and vegetables, you might really want to get into it. Small home dehydrators are available, inexpensive, and easy to use. I love mine, and I know it saves me *many* dollars and much space.

I think that of all the things I store on my "fruit room" shelves, my favorite is my homemade pie filling. This easy recipe is sure a time saver! A tart, juicy cooking apple works best.

I hope you are making lots of jams and jellies. Be sure and save all those cute little jars from mustard, olives, etc. through the year. They make pretty little gifts filled with homemade jam and sealed. A decorative homemade label gives a finishing touch.

When you use your jam and jelly, remove the wax on top, wash it good, and store it in a little container in your fruit room. It can be used over and over; don't waste

CANNED PIE FILLING

Combine: in large kettle
          4 cups sugar
          1 cup cornstarch
          3 tsp. cinnamon
          1 tsp. nutmeg

          1 tsp. salt
Add: 10 cups water

Cook until thickened and add:
          3 T. lemon juice

Fill canning jars 1/3 full of sauce. Peel and slice apples into jars, smooshing down into the sauce until the jar is full.

Put on hot lids, and process in boiling water bath for 20 minutes. Fills 7 quart jars.

When you want to make a pie, just roll out the crust, pour in the filling, dot with butter, and cover with the top crust. Bake at 400 degrees for 40-50 minutes.

You can also substitute other fruits such as peaches or cherries. You may want to vary the spices a little. Sometimes I use a little more cinnamon and nutmeg with apples.

it. I also have a container I keep all my candle stubs in. There are many uses for these throughout the book. Remember, waste not, want not.

Speaking of saving things in my fruit room, as you peel oranges, let the peelings dry on a paper sack and when they are brittle, toss them into a bag (the ones you don't use for the beauty tips in Chapter 2). They are great to throw on the fire on cool fall or winter days.

Also while you are enjoying all that good corn on the cob in the summer, let the corn cobs dry out real well and store these in the garage or garbage bags (*after* they are dried out) near the wood pile. They make great kindling. On our farm in Nebraska, my daily job in the winter was to keep the bushel baskets by the stove full of cobs to start the fires. It really works and has a nice aroma. Just be sure your cobs are dry so they don't mold. We gather all the pine cones we can find in the fall to store in garbage bags for kindling, too.

As I finish up my canning for the season, it's time to bring in herbs. Cut them off leaving about one-third of the stem; be sure to cut before they flower, preferably on a dry day in the afternoon. You may want to shake them off, or wash them. Tie them in bundles and hang in a well-ventilated, dry room. I hang mine from the beams in the ceiling of my huge, old-fashioned kitchen keeping room. They look pretty and smell so good. It usually takes about two weeks until they are completely dry. Then you can crumble them into containers. I like to leave some of mine hanging up, though, for effect and scent.

As I package my herbs, I always make a good supply of my super taco seasoning mix. We use it all the time. Sure saves a bunch of money, too.

You will have so much fun using all the herbs you grow. One decorative way is the herb wreaths I describe in Chapter 8.

If you planted that lavender I suggested, crush some and make little dreamy pillows to lay on your bed. Ummm! they smell so sweet and good. You can also do this with crushed mint leaves. Wouldn't your house

MEXICAN TACO SEASON MIX

Mix together:
- 1/4 cup dried minced onion flakes
- 4 tsp. cornstarch
- 3 T. salt
- 4 T. chili powder
- 3 tsp. cumin
- 1 1/2 tsp. oregano
- 3 tsp. dried minced garlic
- 3 tsp. hot crushed red peppers
- 2 tsp. beef bouillon

Store in tight container.
2 T. equals 1 commercial package.

CRANBERRY JUICE

Boil 8 cups water and 8 cups cranberries until the skins pop (about 5 minutes).

Strain the juice through a cloth. Don't squeeze the bag or you will get sediment in your juice; just let it drip through.

Add: 1 1/4 cups sugar to the juice.

Boil for 2 minutes.

Pour into sterile jars and seal with hot lids.

You can process for 15 minutes in boiling water bath if desired.

It is so simple and really delicious. Be sure and try some.

guests be pleased to find one on their pillows? Or how about taking one to a friend who is bedridden? It will really perk her up.

My girls always loved to make pomander balls, and I still like to have a few around. All you need for these is an orange, whole cloves and other spices. Stick whole cloves in the orange until it is covered. Then roll it in a mixture of cinnamon, nutmeg, allspice and some orris root, which you can buy at the drug store. The proportions of the spices don't matter, just use whatever you have. Roll the clove-covered orange in the spice mixture, shake well to remove excess, and put them in closets and drawers. They last almost forever and smell terrific. If you give a pomander away, good will come to you all year.

Fall is also the time for the cranberry crop. Most of us don't live in an area where they grow, but we can still save lots of money by buying the berries. I make dozens of quarts of cranberry juice every year because it's so full of important vitamins. Roy and Mark drink this by the jar full.

It is so simple and really delicious. Be sure and try some.

Another reason I love the fall is that fall is wheat harvesting time. I hope you have all checked into the fun, economy, and good health with wheat that we discussed in *A Family Raised on Sunshine*. The possibilities with wheat are limitless. I want to share with you a few other wheat recipes people are always asking me for. First, you have got to try making your own Sunshine Wheat Flakes. There is absolutely nothing to

SUNSHINE WHEAT FLAKES

Mix together equal amounts of water and freshly ground whole wheat flour and a pinch of salt.
Stir together well but don't beat.
Pour about 1/4 cup of the mixture onto a teflon-coated lightly greased cookie sheet and tilt the pan around until you get a thin film coating. Pour off any excess.
Bake at 375 degrees for about 15 minutes.
Break up into flakes and store in a plastic bag.

HE-MAN COOKIES

Beat: 3 eggs
Add: 1 cup honey
     1 cup salad oil
     1 whole orange
     (blended in the
     blender)
     1 tsp. vanilla

Mix well and add:
     3 cups whole wheat flour
     4 tsp. baking powder
     2 tsp. cinnamon
     1 1/2 tsp. salt
     1 1/2 cups brown sugar (packed)

Mix together well. Then add:
     2 cups rolled oats
     2 cups wheat germ
Drop by spoonfuls on lightly greased cookie sheet.
Bake at 350 degrees for about 10 minutes.
Don't over bake.

"SUNNY" GRAHAM CRACKERS

Cream together:
>   1 stick margarine
>   2/3 cup brown sugar (packed)

Combine:
>   2 3/4 cups whole wheat flour
>   1/2 tsp. baking powder
>   1/2 tsp. cinnamon

Add alternately with 1/2 cup water to creamed mixture.
Mix well and let dough stand 1/2 hour.
Roll out about 1/4 inch thick on a large greased cookie sheet.
Cut into cracker squares and prick well with a fork.
Bake at 350 degrees for about 12 minutes.
Presto! Your own crackers hot and homemade!

WHEAT CHILI

Brown: 1 lb. ground beef
>   1 chopped onion
>   1 clove garlic (minced)

Add: 2 1-lb. cans kidney beans
>   2 cups steamed wheat
>   4 cups tomatoes and juice
>   1 T. chili powder
>   2 T. brown sugar
>   Dash of cumin
>   Salt and pepper as desired

Simmer together for 1 hour.   Serves 6.

making it, and the kids think it's fantastic. And you'll have a delicious cold breakfast cereal made with nothing but good, pure ingredients.

You can also use a "squirt" bottle and make little shapes or designs on the cookie sheet. Let the kids create your own family cereal. It couldn't be better for you!

Everyone loves our He-Man Cookies, and they are about as healthy as a cookie can get. (They're nice and moist, too.) Give them a try.

Since you have this nice, fresh wheat flour (I hope you are grinding your own), you have to try making your own graham crackers. You'll be so proud!

Now, remember how we "steamed" our whole-wheat kernels? Well, if you have some steamed wheat in your jar in the fridge, here's a delicious dish for supper that is a great budget helper, and all your family will be asking for more.

It's amazing how much better we feel and happier we are as a family when we eat right.

Of course fall is apple time, and in addition to the pie filling on your shelves, be sure and keep a good supply of eating apples. Our favorite is the Melrose apple. Since Roy likes Jonathan, and I like Delicious, this is a great choice for us because it's a combination of these two kinds.

When you bring in the pumpkins and squash, remember you can just cut them up and take the seeds out to dry. Then bake the pieces in the oven all at one time at 375 degrees until tender. When they are done, scoop the "meat" out into meal-sized bags and pop them into the freezer. Then when you want to eat it, just set the frozen squash on a pie plate in a 400 degree oven until heated through. Or you can use it in pies or other recipes.

For another taste treat and inexpensive delicacy, try roasting your pumpkin seeds. Wash the seeds well, then boil them in salted water (about two tablespoons per quart of water) for twenty minutes. Drain well, pat dry with a paper towel, and spread out on a well-buttered cookie sheet. Roast at 350 degrees until they are crisp and nicely browned. Then drizzle a little butter over them and sprinkle with seasoning salt. Boy! are they good.

The good foods you harvest and preserve in the fall will be yours to enjoy when the snow is blowing and winter is here again. But, gardening never stops at our house. I always keep a milk carton under my kitchen sink, and into it I put all the things that would normally go down a garbage disposal—eggshells, vegetable scraps, peels, etc. Every day or two, I run out and throw it into my compost pile or garden. Be sure and cover it well, and soon it will make a rich addition to your soil.

One of the best ways to enjoy your yard in the winter is by having a bird feeder or two. Steve built two of them for us out of scrap lumber, and we have continuous entertainment out of our bay window. (Sometimes I get so intrigued watching the birds and squirrels I forget I have work to do.)

One of our feeders is mainly for the squirrels, and they are really a riot to watch. We fill our squirrel feeder with the coarser kinds of foods and set it where the squirrels can reach it easily (thus they're less likely to bother the bird feeders, which we place in more precarious spots). We've gotten so well acquainted with the squirrels that they each have a name. First, there is "Piggy." He thinks he owns the place, and he chases all the others away. He eats until he is so fat he can hardly get up the tree. Little "Mama" is kind of timid and waits her turn when "Piggy" is around. "Itchy" is pretty little so he waits in the trees until everyone else is out of sight. He must have fleas, though, or maybe he is just nervous; but he is scratching all the time. "The Friends" are the playful ones. They sure have lots of ambition. They are always playing games and chasing one another. They come to eat together, too. These five squirrels have kept us entertained all through the winter.

Our bird feeder is busy all the time, too, and we've noticed that the birds each prefer to eat at different times of the day. My favorite bird to watch is the cardinal. They always come in pairs to feed and take turns keeping watch while the other eats. They are real nervous birds, but their colors are so beautiful—they almost look artificial.

We have found that the favorite feed for most birds is a mixed seed, or wheat, sunflower seeds, or cracked corn. Not too many enjoy milo, millet, or peanut hearts.

One thing you have to remember, though, is that once you start feeding birds in the winter, don't stop. They become dependent on you and will die rather than find other food. Also, it's a good idea to keep up your feeding program the year 'round. Your yard will stay most active this way. Just make sure that there is somewhere close by that they can fly to for shelter in a hurry if they need to.

For some really enjoyable times at your house, build a bird feeder today. You'll learn so much and see a different show every day. And, after the show, just settle back and enjoy the seed catalogs and your house plants. The very best tip I can give you for your house plants is to keep a squirt bottle filled with water, and every morning as you are straightening up the house, give each plant (with the exception of cactus and African Violets) a spray mist of water. They will love you for it.

Add a touch of green to your family's rainbow and reap a harvest of happy memories.

7
Happy Days Called Holidays

Not many of us have a "Mary Poppins" at our house to make "every day a holiday." But with a little positive thinking, a genuine love for ourselves and our families, and that trusty old smile, we can make any day special. Sometimes I think that is why there are holidays on the calendar every so often. It jogs our memories and helps us put forth a little more effort toward happiness for others.

Any opportunity we have to show our children the joys of sharing and giving should be taken advantage of. We start our New Year out by having a little celebration as we take down the Christmas tree. Stephen carries the gingerbread house that we have been enjoying through the holidays out into the backyard and puts it up in a branch of the tree near our bay window. Then as we enjoy our meals, we watch the birds enjoying the gingerbread house. It is so much fun to see how excited the birds get. They peek in the door and peck away on the chimney. We also set our Christmas tree in the backyard, leaving the strings of popcorn and cranberries on it, and the birds take refuge in its branches well into the spring. Then we saw

up the tree for firewood, and nothing goes to waste.

Since January is kind of a slow, quiet month, it is a great time to have a holiday for each member of the family. Why not have a "We're thankful for Billy" day? Each member of the family needs to feel wanted, and it's so fun to surprise them (like on "This Is Your Life") by having a day or evening set aside just for them. When we did this in our home, we would each tell something we liked about the person, sing some of his favorite songs, and play the games he liked best. Then we would have a mini-movie looking at the slides with him from birth until the current time. Often we would each give the person a present of a promise to do something special with or for the individual being honored that week. Then, of course, we ended the evening with his favorite treat. Declare a holiday for someone in your family this week.

As you know, I'm an old sentimentalist, so I love Valentine's Day. This is one of the best times to make someone a Happiness Note Jar. (See Chapter 2.)

Our basic gingerbread house (see Chapter 8) can provide lots of fun hours

I love you this much.

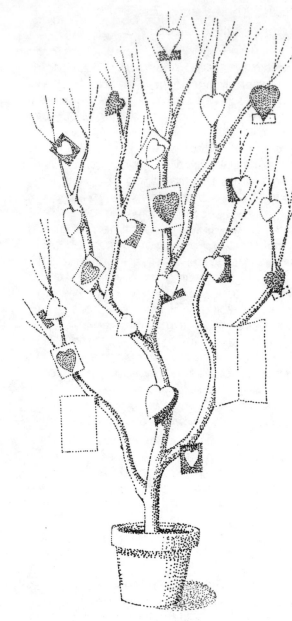

creating a decorative touch for any holiday. Try making it lacy and frilly looking with "red hots," red licorice heart-shaped candies, red gumdrops and icing for Valentine's Day.

It makes a cute little Irish bungalow decorated with spaghum moss, shamrocks, and icing; the look of a log cabin graced with a cherry tree for President's Day, and even an eerie spook house for Halloween complete with icing ghosts, thread cobwebs, black licorice bats, candy pumpkins, and miniature cornstalks.

Here's a Valentine's Day present I made for our youngest daughter, Heidi, who has always had so much love for everyone. We always got a kick out of asking her, when she was little, how much she loved someone. She would stretch her arms just as wide as she could and say, "This much!" Since this is her first year away from home, at college, I made her this to decorate her bed. It is so cute. I cut out the pillow shape from brushed velour for a soft feeling and drew the features in with a permanent marking pencil, then stuffed with leftover quilt batting. Maybe you would like to make one for your someone special.

Every house should have a valentine tree. These are so easy to make. Just go out and find a small, sturdy branch with lots of tiny little branches on it. Then spray it with white paint. (Be sure you do this in a well ventilated room.) When the paint is completely dry, "plant" it in a clay flowerpot filled with sand or pebbles. You can tie a bow around the pot or cover it with foil or wrapping paper. Then the kids can attach their valentines with a little transparent tape, and it makes such a pretty decoration in the house. Everyone loves to trim a tree, and you'll find that you can use it over and over and over again. Decorate it with green bows and shamrocks in March, with colored eggshells for Easter, flags for July 4, as a centerpiece for a baby shower using little flannel diapers fastened with gold safety pins, or flowers and little gold rings for a bridal shower, and then, of course, ghosts and pumpkins at Halloween, and...you'll have the tree worn out before you run out of ideas.

Let me tell you some more good ideas for bridal showers. Since so many young couples today enjoy plants and growing things, how about a "garden" shower? The invitations can be on a little packet of seeds; games and favors involving the garden; have the guests bring gifts to help the couple get started with a vegetable garden—a tool, seeds, watering hose, sprinkler, special bulbs, "how to" books on gardens, etc. With today's inflation, you couldn't give a newlywed couple a better start.

Young people now are also realizing the importance of sewing, and this craft can also make a fun subject for a shower. Gifts and decorations can be planned around this. And, here is a "sewing" game to play:

Hints for a Happy Marriage

You will find you will have to have (red) your cookbook very well, so never try to pull the (wool) over his eyes, because he can tell the difference between a (white) cake and a (sponge) cake. Never be guilty of telling him a (yarn) or you will find yourself in a (net) for sure. He won't want to find his chair (satin) or his pockets (felt) in. So you should (print) your love firmly in his heart. He will love you for ever and ever and probably take you to (Jersey) on a honeymoon and call you his (cream puff or whipped cream — the fabric, not the food!) Together (lace) the (string) of love so firmly that not even a (thread) may fray loose.

Tiny swatches of different types of fabric are passed out in little bags together with this word puzzle. Each little swatch represents a word to fill in a blank.

This game can be adapted to any party; a birthday party, baby shower, or even an anniversary party. Just write up different little rules or ideas still using fabrics or small items taped to the paper to fill in for the words.

It's also fun to have an "old-fashioned" shower. Decorate with some antique household items, have hot homemade bread and jams for refreshments, and bring gifts that are "back to basics." The secret to planning a party is first to have a theme. Then be as creative as you can be and think of games, decorations, and gifts to fit your theme.

Since I enjoy cooking so much, my favorite theme is "Look What's Cooking" (a wedding, a birth, a birthday, an anniversary, anything!). Send out a recipe that you will be serving at the party but tear it in half. Tell your guests to come and get the other half. Then you can print the invitation details on the reverse side. I have even cut out little aprons with pinking shears and slipped the invitation in a little pocket. If the apron invitation were to a

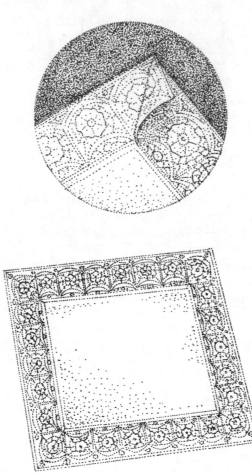

wedding shower, all gifts could be kitchen utensils.

I have a little idea for a gift that I love to make for a new bride. Every bride should have a pretty handkerchief to carry, but these can be quite expensive. I watch for sales on lace trims and remnants of a fine batiste to make them myself. They are so simple. They sew up in a few minutes and look very elegant and impressive. Just cut a square of the fabric a little larger than you desire the center of the hanky to be (about an eight-inch square). Then cut four strips of wide lace the length of the side of the square plus enough to overlap each lace strip on the sides. Pin the strips to the square of fabric overlapping about one-half inch on the outer edge of the square, and allowing the strips of lace to completely overlap each other at the corners. If you have a prominent flower in the lace, try to match them on top of each other on the corner also. Then with a tiny, close-together, zigzag stitch, stitch around the outside of the square of fabric securing the lace. Then stitch down each corner of the lace on an angle. With a pair of little scissors, trim away excess fabric next to the lace along the stitching, and also excess lace on each corner, making a perfect mitered corner! It is so fast and easy, you'll be making them by the dozens. I even like to make them for the bridesmaids and mothers with a pastel lace. By the way, this is also a great way to trim napkins, doilies, and tablecloths. It's the fastest and neatest way of edging I have ever found, and it looks so professional.

Be sure you watch for all the trimming specials. I always keep a drawer full. For a few cents, they really add elegance to a gift. Lace and crochet-trimmed bath towels are the rage now and you really pay a fortune for a set. I just stock up on towels during the white sales in January. Then I can combine them with my "sale" laces and trims for an impressive gift. Just stitch the laces to the towel with a zigzag stitch, and be sure to tuck the ends under for a neat, finished look. Use the color of the lace as your top thread color, and the

bits of raisin (or currants) for his eyes and a carrot tip for a beak. They look so cute sitting on a plate. With one or two of them on a slice of ham, a fruit cup, a hot-cross bun, and a glass of milk, the family will be delighted.

Speaking of hot-cross buns, they are so much fun to have for Easter, expensive to buy but easy to make. Why not try some for your family? It is really just a variation of my sweet roll recipe.

For Easter dinner we always have ham, and the best way to serve ham for a holiday in our German home is with *Mehlbeutel*. This is the German word for "big dumpling." It is an unusual meal, very traditionally German and absolutely fantastic. When I prepare this dish on a television show, the crew just can't get enough. The big dumpling is steamed in a kettle (when I was a little girl, we wrapped the dough in a clean dish towel and dropped it in boiling water. It is still cooked this way in Germany.) Our oldest son, Stephen, spent two years in Germany on a mission for our church and was always thrilled when someone invited him over for *Mehlbeutel*.

While the dumpling is steaming, you cook a pan of dried stewed fruit and brown two sticks of butter and two sticks of margarine together. Then at meal time each person is served a generous slice of baked ham and a slice of the dumpling with the browned butter drizzled over and a nice serving of the stewed fruit on top. That's it! No other accompaniments. It's a complete meal. Here's the recipe.

To bake ham, use a butt or shank portion with the bone in (the butt end is the best buy). Place it on a baking rack in a pan

color of the towel as your bobbin thread color. You'll never even see the stitching. You can even combine several trims on one towel for a striking look. Be creative!

Spring is always a kind of festive time. After being inside so much in the winter, we are all anxious to see things growing and get reacquainted with our neighbors and friends. Easter seems to mark the beginning of this feeling of reawakening. With all the new little buds, flowers, and leaves, our creative ideas really start to blossom also.

It's fun to start Easter morning by serving hard-cooked eggs as little chicks. Cut the white of each egg in half, being careful not to cut the yolk. Then with the whole yolk sitting in the half of white, it becomes the head of a little chick. You can use two little

HOT CROSS BUNS

Dissolve: 1 pkg. dry yeast in 1/4 cup warm water.

Scald: 1 cup milk.

Add: 1 stick margarine (so it melts)
1/2 cup sugar
1 1/2 tsp. salt
Combine yeast mixture with milk mixture when the milk has cooled.

Add: 3 beaten eggs

Stir in: 4 3/4 cups flour
1 tsp. cinnamon
1 tsp. grated lemon peel

Stir with spoon until dough is smooth (it will be sticky).

Add: 1 cup chopped raisins or currants

Cover bowl with a damp towel and let rise in a warm place until double.

When double, stir down. Then turn dough onto a floured board.

Shape into balls about the size of an egg.

Place on greased cookie sheet (about 2-3 inches apart) and let rise until almost double again.

Brush tops with beaten egg white.

Bake at 375 degrees until nicely browned (12-15 minutes).

When cool, pipe frosting across the top in the shape of a cross.

FROSTING

Stir together: 1 cup powdered sugar
1 T. margarine
1/2 tsp. lemon extract
enough hot water to make desired consistency.

MEHLBEUTEL

Cream
together: 1 cup margarine
2/3 cup sugar
Add: 4 eggs — one at a
time.

Sift: 4 1/2 cups flour
1 tsp. salt
4 tsp. baking pow-
der

Add alternately with 2 cups milk.
Then stir in 1 cup raisins or currants.
This makes enough for 10 people, so you may need to steam it in two batches. Count on It doubling in size as it steams.
Put the dough into a container and set in steamer.
Steam for 2 hours.
Meanwhile, brown:
2 sticks butter
2 sticks margarine in a saucepan.
Also, cover a 12-oz. bag of dried mixed fruit, a package of prunes, and some dried apples with water. Stew together until tender. Thicken with a little cornstarch if desired. Any combination of dried fruits can be used.

with the *cut*-side down. Don't glaze. Bake in a 325 degree oven for two and a half to three hours if it's about eight to ten pounds. If the ham is precooked, it just needs to be well-heated through.

You will have a feast you'll long remember!

While we are talking about ham, and it is really one of the more economical meats, we *always* cook our ham plain. Everyone always says what a good flavor it has, and I think it's because most people hide that true ham flavor with fancy glazings and basting sauces.

If we have a traditional baked ham dinner, I do make a raisin sauce to serve over the slices at the table. It really is good, but it doesn't mask the ham flavor.

RAISIN SAUCE

Melt: 2 T. butter
 Stir: in 2 T. flour
 Add: 2 cups apple cider
        1/2 cup raisins

Bring to a boil, stirring constantly. Simmer for 2 minutes. Serve hot!

Speaking of covering up flavors with glazes, etc., most people do the same thing with yams. We love yams at our house, but why bury them beneath sweet syrup and marshmallows? Next time just scrub them well and bake them at 375 degrees for one to one and a half hours. Then just scoop them out on your plate and put some butter on the top. The flavor can't be beat, and everyone always says how great the yams taste. Too many times we forget the simple way is best!

In the summer time most of our holidays are spent outside, and there are exciting ideas to make those happy days, too. I can remember as a child begging my mother to let us eat outside under the trees. When my children came along, they were the same way. There is just something magic in eating our meals outdoors. Everything tastes better. It's just like hot dogs at a ball game. They never taste the same anywhere else.

In serving a meal outside, the first thing we have to do is prepare the table. Let me give you a little hint that has saved many a catastrophe. Just glue one side of a clip clothespin to the underneath side of each corner of your picnic table. You can then just pinch the cloth in the clothespin on the corners and nothing blows away! It works great!

We especially like root-beer floats in the summer with our picnics, but we try to avoid buying "pop." So I really appreciate my friend's, Marge Reeve Emery, recipe for quick homemade root beer. (I'm sure you feel like you know Marge by now. Her name keeps popping up in my books. She is always so willing to help someone learn. So many of you have shared ideas with me, and through ideas our list of friends grows and grows.)

If you haven't ever tasted homemade root beer, be prepared for a different taste; it's terrific.

Another fun idea for entertaining outside is to purchase a piece of white oil cloth

MARGE'S ROOT BEER

Dissolve: 1 tsp. dry yeast in 1/2
cup warm water.
Add: 2 cups sugar
2 T. root beer extract

Put into gallon jar.
Fill the rest of the jar with lukewarm water, put a lid on it, and let it stand at room temperature for 12 hours. Then refrigerate until well chilled.
Serve with a scoop of ice cream in each glass.

(get the flannel-backed kind if you can) to use as a tablecloth. Each time you have a guest over, have him sign it with a permanent magic marker. Then you can cover it with a clear plastic tablecloth to protect it while you eat. It's fun to look at it and remember all the guests you've had. You also might like to do this when you give a farewell party for someone. The guest of honor can then take the tablecloth containing the signatures and sentiments of the guests to his or her new home. It's a fun remembrance. The kids like to do this at a slumber party with a plain pillowcase. Everyone autographs it with a permanent marker. Just be sure to slip a piece of cardboard inside so the ink doesn't soak through.

When we entertain in the summer, the key is to keep it simple (shouldn't it always be?). When I look at all of the elegant entertaining dishes in magazines, I always wonder if people really do all that fancy stuff for a picnic. I'm afraid I would be a nervous wreck and would make everyone else nervous, too. Or worse yet, I'd just never invite anyone over. I always feel that entertaining is getting together to enjoy one another's company and not to give an "on stage" cooking show. Don't you think our world needs more friendships and less struggles to impress?

Here are two of our favorite Mexican casserole-type dishes that are super simple to put together. With a tossed salad, corn chips, and tomato salsa hot dip, these are great for an evening with friends.

I love the fall season, too. Again, it's a

LOIS'S CHILI RELLENO CASSEROLE

Beat: 4 egg whites until stiff. Fold in 2 T. flour.
Combine: (and beat well) 1 13-oz. can evaporated milk.
4 egg yolks

Fold yolk mixture into whites mixture.
In a 9x13 inch pan, alternate layers of:
1 lb. cheddar cheese, shredded
1 lb. Monterey Jack cheese, shredded
2 4-oz. cans chopped green chilies
Pour egg mixture over layers.
Top with 2 8-oz. cans of tomato sauce.
Bake at 325 degrees for about 1 hour.
Serves 8.

change of pace. After the carefree outdoor days of summer, I start feeling like the squirrels. Time to get my nest ready for winter and the holidays ahead. With all my food shelves stocked again with goodies from our garden, we can look forward to the festive days of fall and winter.

Don't forget to take time to relax and enjoy the beautiful fall leaves. Two of our favorite things about this pretty city of Cincinnati are the hills and the unbelievably beautiful autumn leaves. I never knew there were so many varieties and colors.

If you would like to prepare some colorful leaves for Thanksgiving decorating, just gather them, dip into melted wax, dry on brown paper sacks, and they will keep for a long time.

Another thing I like to do especially with big leathery, dark-green leaves is to crush the end of the stem with a hammer, then stand them in a mixture of half water and half glycerine for about two weeks. This mixture is drawn up into the leaves, and

NOODLES MEXICANO

Brown: 1 lb. ground beef.
   Add: 1 large onion, chopped
        2 cloves garlic, minced
        1/2 green pepper,
        chopped
        1 tsp. salt
        Cook until tender.

Add: 1 lb. can of corn and the
      liquid
      6 oz. pitted olives sliced
      and liquid
      1/2 lb. dry noodles
      1 fat can tomatoes
      1 tsp. chili powder

Mix together.
Cover and cook on low heat for 1/2 hour. Remove cover, sprinkle on 1/2 lb. grated cheese and cover again. Return to low heat for 5 minutes and serve.
Serves 6.

they stay soft and pliable for a long time. They are so pretty to use in decorating for the holidays.

Halloween somehow makes fall official. I love to smell the bonfires, the crispy apples in the orchards, and as funny as it may seem, the dried cornstalks in the fields. Somehow it gives me the feeling that everything and everybody have done their duty, and all is right with the world.

Roy and I always like the feeling of festivity that is in the air on Halloween. We get almost as excited as the kids. We spent days before, preparing costumes — everything from sewing fancy clown suits, to gathering old jewelry for gypsies, to finding large boxes for robots, to the time I was in the hospital and Roy very realistically dressed the little boys up in his old soldier outfits right down to the bandages and "catsup" blood. Boy, did they think they were hot stuff!

I always tried to make dinner a little special yet simple that night because everyone was anxious to get dressed up and go out. You can serve a fun Halloween meal by making stew and baking it in a cleaned-out real pumpkin. I brown a cut-up round steak or whatever is on special (stew meat is much higher and not nearly so lean and good). I use a hot pan and no grease. Put the cut-up meat in the pan and turn the heat down a little; the juices and fats from the meat will loosen the meat, and you can turn it over after it's seared and browned on one side. After the meat is well-browned, I salt and pepper it and add about one and a half quarts of *hot* water, a piece of celery, some onion, a bay leaf, and cover the pan. Let it simmer all day. Then mix three tablespoons cornstarch in about one-half cup cold water and stir into the *strained* broth. Stir until thickened, return the pieces of meat to the thickened gravy, and add one cup each cooked carrots, corn, green beans, limas if desired, cut-up *cooked* potatoes, and maybe a few tomatoes. The vegetable choice is up to your family preference. Just be sure they are precooked. If you cook the vegetables, especially the carrots and potatoes, in the stew broth, you lose lots of your rich flavor. I like to wrap some potatoes in foil and bake them ahead of time when I have the oven on anyway. Then I just peel off the foil and cut them up in my stew, peeling and all. The flavor is great. (This is the same way I make my soup, only I increase the water to three quarts and don't use any thickening.)

Now after you have made your stew (you can make it a day ahead — it tastes even better), put it into a cleaned-out small pumpkin and bake it at 375 degrees for about one and a half to two hours depending on the size of the pumpkin.

GERMAN SCONES

Dissolve: 2 pkgs. dry yeast in 1/2
　　　　　cup warm water.
Add: 1 T. sugar
Pour: 1 cup boiling water
　　　over:
　　　　　1/2 cup sugar

　　　　　1/2 cup margarine
　　　　　2 tsp. salt
Add: 3 beaten eggs
　　　Yeast mixture
　　　2 cups flour

Beat with mixer until smooth.
　　Add: 2 1/2 cups flour and stir in.
Let rise for 1 hour, then refrigerate.
When desired, roll out very thin and cut in 2-inch squares. Fry in hot fat.

When the pumpkin "meat" is tender, it is ready to serve. As you scoop out the stew and serve it, you also get pieces of the baked pumpkin. Tastes just like squash and makes a delicious meal.

Another fun way to serve a small pumpkin is to clean out the seeds and fill the center with a mixture of apple slices, a few raisins, one-half to one cup sugar, and two teaspoons cinnamon, one teaspoon nutmeg, a dash of ginger and cloves, and a few chopped nuts. Bake at 375 degrees for about one and a half to two hours until the apples and pumpkin meat are tender. Scoop out and serve in dishes topped with ice cream or half-and-half. Yummy! is that good—tastes like hot apple and pumpkin pie combined!

While the kids were growing up, we were transferred quite often, so we discovered a way to meet our new neighbors on Halloween. You'll have lots of fun doing this. On your front porch, set up a card table with your electric skillet and start frying some hot German scones. Have some apple cider handy, also. Then as the neighbors bring their little ones around "trick or treating," instead of standing out by the curb they can come up and have a hot scone and a cup of warm cider while their children get their treat. It's really a fun way to get acquainted. It's also a nice "warm" pause for them on a sometimes chilly fall evening.

Soon Thanksgiving rolls around, and everyone is feeling creative anticipating the holiday celebrations. Again, use things around the house, keep things simple and family-oriented. It means so much more to everyone and builds memories. *Anyone* can buy a few cutouts, ornaments, or decorations at the store and set them out. That isn't any fun.

Our traditional centerpiece through Thanksgiving-time is our easy-to-make fresh pineapple "turkey" surrounded with apples and nuts, stems of wheat, and things of the harvest time. Just use a pineapple lying on its side as the body of the turkey with the green leaves on top, making the tail. The head is cut from two pieces of felt, sewn together part way and pinned on with two straight pins. It lasts for quite a while, smells good, and you can use the head over next year.

The kids always liked to make individual table place name markers out of pine cones. The pine cone was the turkey body, then with construction paper we made a wide tail with the person's name printed on to put on the flat end of the pine cone, stood the pine cone on its side, and made a neck and head to paste on the tapered end.

Cute turkeys can also be made out of an apple turned on its side. Thread about eight to ten raisins on each toothpick and use about five toothpicks fanned out to form a tail. Little marshmallows on a toothpick make his neck with a big marshmallow for his head. His "goggler" is a few raisins on a short toothpick, whole cloves make his eyes, and a piece of raisin forms a beak. The kids will have lots of fun creating.

Nearly everyone has turkey at Thanksgiving, and it is a good buy this time of year, so stock you freezer with several. Always buy the biggest one you can get. A turkey can only have so many bones, and after about twelve pounds, you're getting nearly all meat for your money. Don't worry if your family is small. It is still the best buy, and you won't have to eat turkey for days on end. Here's the way I do it, and I think it's one of the most exciting ideas I've had.

I ask the butcher to saw it in half for me crosswise then lengthwise. They look at me kinda funny but always do it anyway. Then when I get home, I bag each quarter separately. Those two front halves are just like perfect white-meat roasters. Sometimes I bake one with stuffing (if I have accumulated lots of leftover toast and bread) or I bake it on a rack with cream of chicken soup poured over it. I may just bake it and slice it for sandwiches, or our favorite way is baked and basted with barbeque sauce. Mmm! It's so tender, it just melts in your mouth.

I have a special use for those two back halves. I put one in my big soup kettle, cover it with five or six quarts of water, celery, carrots, and an onion, salt, and pepper. Then I just let it cook and simmer all day. In the evening, I strain the broth, giving me about five nice quarts of broth, and I pick that tender meat off the bones. (Nothing like it if it had been roasted). I put the meat in five separate plastic bags, and I have a bag of meat for each quart of broth. Now I freeze these, and it's so simple to pull out a bag of meat and a jar of broth to make chicken and noodles, chicken and dumplings, chicken (whoops, I mean turkey!) and rice, or a meat pie or casserole. You can have such varied meals with such a little work, and save lots of grocery money, too.

We all have house guests over the holidays, and it's always been a choice time for our family to try and bring a little brightness and color to someone else's life. We always try to have a few good books or magazines in the guest room, a dish of nuts or fruits to nibble on, and maybe even a pretty flower or two if we are fortunate to have some blooming. It makes the guest feel special and cared about, and gives our kids a chance to enjoy making someone happy. One word of caution, though: Save a few tasks until your company comes. Don't break your neck trying to do "everything" and be worn out and dead tired. Company likes to feel useful and can really enjoy helping in the festivities. Baking cookies or decorating *together* can be lots more fun.

By the way, when you are rushing around doing that last-minute cleaning, slip some old socks over the legs of your heavy furniture. It makes them slide lots better and won't mar your wood floors.

Do what you can to prepare and then just enjoy your guests when they arrive. Don't be a martyr—put on your smile and enjoy them every minute. Happy holidays are the bright gold ray in our family's rainbow. I hope yours will glisten just like ours.

8
The Year-Round Gift of Christmas

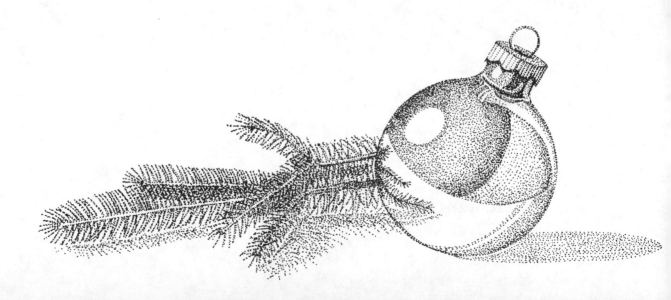

Christmas at our house is like our yard and gardening—it's a year-round thing. There's a special drawer in the house where I tuck little gifts for people as I find them on sale through the year. It's also a continuous search for decorating and gift ideas that we can make ourselves. I nearly always have an afghan or quilt in the works. These are my "frustration" projects. When I'm tired or tense about something, I can work on one of these for a little while, and it really relaxes me. It's also something I can pick up when I have a few minutes of waiting time. We all need something like this. The end result makes a nice gift, too.

We have four set traditions at Christmas. First, we always choose a theme to carry out in our decorating. Second, we try to *make* as many gifts as possible. Third, we have a traditional list of goodies that we make every year. And fourth, we have a traditional way in which we observe the actual holiday.

First let's talk about decorating. This is the part of the holiday that really sets the mood and gets everyone into the spirit of things. We have always thought it was easier and more fun to decorate if we chose a central theme. Our favorite is the gingerbread idea. Everyone should make a ginger-

ROYAL ICING

Mix
together: 3 egg whites
(room temperature)
1/2 tsp. cream of tartar
1 lb. powdered sugar

Beat until it stands in peaks.
Keep bowl covered with a damp towel to keep the icing from drying.
A little water or more powdered sugar may be added to get the right consistency.

GINGERBREAD

Mix
together: 1/2 cup oil
1/3 cup brown sugar
(packed)
Add: 1 egg
2/3 cup molasses

Then add: 2 3/4 cups flour
3 tsp. baking powder
1/2 tsp. salt
1 tsp. ginger
1 tsp. cinnamon
1/8 tsp. cloves

Mix well and chill overnight.
Roll dough out on lightly oiled foil to fit a 12x7 inch jelly roll-size pan.
Don't roll too thick.
Use any excess dough for gingerbread boys.
Bake at 300 degrees for 20-30 minutes.
Have pattern pieces ready, remove gingerbread from oven, and cut around pattern pieces immediately. It will be too hard to cut when cool. (If necessary, the pieces can be put back in the oven to harden. They will not hold up if they are soft.)
When thoroughly cool, cover a piece of cardboard with foil on which to place the gingerbread house. Mix up royal icing.

bread house. They are so simple, and you can really be creative. It also gives your house the most delightful smell. We start making ours about Thanksgiving time. This way we can enjoy ours all through the holiday season, and have plenty of time to make several for friends, too. Here is my best gingerbread-house recipe.

To assemble: With a decorating tube, draw a wide line on the foil-covered cardboard. Stand one side of the house upright in it. Put a line of icing across the back and down the end of the side piece to fasten the back of the house on to. Repeat the procedure and put on the other side, then the front, and finally the roof pieces. Remember to always run a strip of icing on the foil to stand each piece in and also up the side to cement to the next piece. You'll be surprised how easily it goes together.

Then the fun part begins. With your decorating tip, you can draw on windows and designs, and cover your "seams." We also use little gumdrops, candy canes, red hots, and hard candies. Animal crackers, popcorn, life savers, and jelly beans can be cleverly used too. Don't forget the little door. Finish off with icicles hanging from the eaves. This is my trademark. All of my houses have icicles hanging on them. They are really so easy to make. With a small writing tip, squeeze a little icing on the roof edge. Then just keep squeezing as you draw away from the roof until it falls as an icicle. Try it—you'll soon be an expert.

I use only two decorating tips—about a number 4 writing tube and a 31 fluted tube. They work just fine. You'll soon be making gingerbread houses for all your friends and neighbors and be so proud of your work.

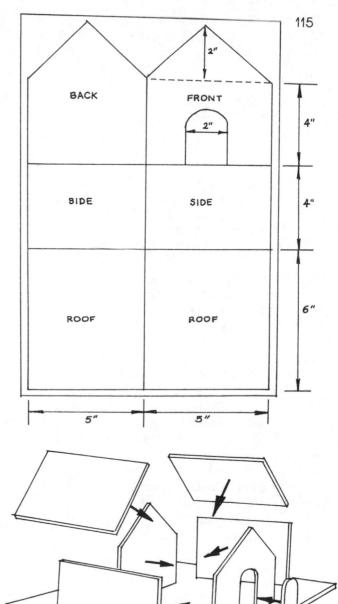

Gingerbread House

Cute little evergreen trees can also be made by putting four small gumdrops on a little mound of icing. Squirt a little more icing on top of the gumdrops, add three gumdrops, a little more icing, and one gumdrop on top.

Fences are fun to make, too. These can be made from gumdrops, red hots, miniature marshmallows, or—our favorite—red licorice. Both the stick and rope varieties can be used. Marshmallows also make neat snowmen.

I like to make fences by stacking three miniature marshmallows on a dab of icing every two to three inches and then draping red string licorice between each little stack to resemble the fence boards.

A cobblestone fence can be made by using "rock" candy and icing as the cement or a simulated brick wall can be done with sugar cubes brushed with red food coloring diluted in a little water.

Cinnamon sticks or pretzel sticks create a real rustic-looking fence also.

While you're making your gingerbread houses, try putting together some miniature houses with graham cracker squares. They are easy to put together and look cute hanging on the tree. Just assemble the graham cracker squares as you would the gingerbread pieces for a house.

Be sure you also make plenty of gingerbread boys and girls and toys or animal cookies, too, from the gingerbread piped in icing. I always have a bunch hanging on my cookie tree in the kitchen, in the windows, on the tree, etc. In fact, just gingerbread cookies, little apples, and red gingham bows with twinkley lights sure make a pretty tree.

If you stick little gingerbread people with names printed on them into shiny red apples, they make cute place cards for Christmas dinner. To do this, bake a toothpick into the bottom of the gingerbread man. The protruding end of the toothpick can be stuck into the apple.

A patriotic theme is also pretty for Christmas. You can trim your tree with red, white, and blue balls or little stuffed ornaments using red and blue bandanas. Trim the ornaments with white eyelet or rickrack. Cut tree skirts can also be made patchwork style from the bandanas. Then add a wintery look with snowmen and snowflakes. Poinsettias are a good accent for a natural theme. I love having big baskets of pine cones and apples by the fireplace, and decorations made from nuts, berries, and dried things. And now it's time to make our wreath from the pods and cones we gathered in Chapter 5.

Cut a piece of one-quarter-inch plywood to the desired shape and size. I usually cut a circle about sixteen inches in diameter with the center cut out. Then coat the board with about one-fourth inch thick covering of linoleum paste. This stays soft for quite awhile. Then start putting on your dried materials. Do the outer and inner edges first. I like to use milo, wheat, or tiny pine cones for the edges. Then fill the major portion of the wreath with larger cones and pods, filling in the little nooks and crannies with the tinier objects. Be sure to press each object into the paste well. They are so fun to make and easy, too. After they are completely set and dry, I spray them with a coat of varnish or a sealer of some kind.

The many natural shades of brown shine through and are really beautiful. Sometimes we make smaller wreaths out of the

Speaking of wreaths, I am kind of a wreath-aholic. I love wreaths all over the house any time of year. My favorite is my calico-bow wreath. These can be done in any color scheme, and look pretty all year long. Start with a doughnut-shaped, round styrofoam wreath form. Cut strips of fabric, with a pinking shears, fourteen inches by one inch. Tie these strips into bows, then with a straight pin through the knot of the bow stick the bow into the wreath. When you add the next bow, hold up both sides

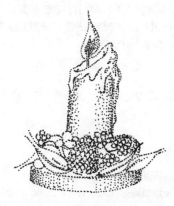

of the first bows so the knots can go right next to one another. The fuller your wreath, the prettier it will be. It takes quite a bit of material, but it's a great way to use up scraps. You don't need to take the bows clear around to the back of the form because you want to hang it flush on the door or wall. These can be just the thing for the sewing room, or done in pastel checks in a baby's room. You can even do them from the bandana print, if you are using that theme.

centers we removed from the larger wreaths. I use these to stand a big candle in as a centerpiece! (Don'l waste a thing, remember?)

If you are using a natural theme, another pretty wreath can be done the same way, using plywood and linoleum paste. Just outline the board and do a design in rope. Then fill in with different kinds of nuts. Finish by spraying with clear varnish.

POPCORN WREATH

It takes about 3 qts. of popped corn to make a nice-sized wreath. Keep popcorn warm in the oven while you make a syrup of —

    1/2 cup white corn syrup
    2/3 cup white sugar
    1/4 tsp. cream of tartar
    dash of salt
    1/4 stick margarine

Stir together in large saucepan until boiling, then cover and boil 2 minutes. It should be to a soft crack stage. Pour over popcorn and shape wreath.

A cute wreath can also be made by covering bottle caps with calico fabric or bright cotton print using a circle of cardboard in the inside to hold the fabric in place. Then mount all of these on a wreath-shaped styrofoam base with white glue, edge with eyelet ruffling, and top with a bow.

Popcorn wreaths are fun to do. You can either make your favorite caramel corn or candied popcorn recipe and shape it into a wreath, or shape it over a styrofoam base. Add red bows and peppermint candies. It's so cheery in a kitchen.

If you started your herb garden this spring, you are ready to make several very aromatic wreaths. Make one for your kitchen door of dried statice, artemisia, yarrow, etc. Just twist a stiff wire in a circle the size you want and twist the ends together. Then stick the ends of the herbs into the twisted ends and start weaving the plant around the circle. Tie it every so often with a piece of twine. Then you can tie on cinnamon sticks, bay leaves, ginger root, dried hot peppers, or little net bags of cloves, nutmeg, or any spices. Or try a trimming of tiny kitchen utensils or bagels, hard rolls, and a few ears of Indian corn.

Even your grapevine trimmings can be fashioned into a wreath and trimmed with a few nuts, apples, and a gingham bow.

Again, take the long trimmings and twist around a heavy wire circle, tying where needed to control ends.

Your Christmas tree is naturally a major part of any theme you choose, but buying a tree can be a real expense. We do prefer a real tree for the fragrant aroma it adds to our house at Christmas time. It gives a warmth that no artificial tree can match. A green, living tree helps us appreciate the things of the earth our Heavenly Father has blessed us with that are so much more beautiful than tinsel and glitter.

Don't think you have to buy the most expensive tree on the lot, though. Pick out that lonely little lopsided one that no one looked at. The bad side can always be put to the wall, and I remember many Christmases when Roy performed major surgery on our tree, taking a spare limb or two from below and very carefully "tying" them into place in bare spots with heavy thread or twine. The twine does not show when the tree is trimmed, so you can just tie the extra branch into place. Those little trees brought our family much enjoyment.

We always give the kids a new tree ornament or two each year to add to their collection, so they will have something to start their own trees with when they are married. These are always indicative of something that happened in their lives that year. The year Heidi got her braces, we got her a tiny stuffed animal with two big front teeth. The year Mark was elected drum major of his band in Texas, he got a little toy soldier marching with his baton.

Lots of ornaments are fun to make, too. Have you ever done the kind you dip in wax? You can use any size styrofoam ball, cover it with a pretty picture cut from magazines or cards, or use seeds and grains in various shapes and designs. When using pictures, the plain, white styrofoam ball can be covered with colored tissue paper first. Cut your pictures out neatly and carefully and cover the styrofoam ball gluing the picture securely as you go. Next, melt paraffin in a tin can and brush on wax in thin coats until the entire ball is well-coated. Use a paring knife to scrape off any thick places. When thoroughly hardened, rub the ball vigorously with an old bath towel for a pretty sheen. If the right pictures are used, these can look very elegant. If you cover the styrofoam balls with seeds, they can just be dipped into the can of melted wax. To use the seeds, coat the styrofoam ball with white glue as you go and lay the different types of seeds and grains on in pretty designs and patterns.

Be sure and save all your felt and fabric scraps to make little stuffed ornaments. Make things to remind the family of fun events of the year. Or maybe use a tiny shell from your vacation glued to a little circle form, a little corncob pig made from a cob saved from canning corn as a family, or a little crocheted snowflake or wreath from the beginning crocheter in your house.

Speaking of snowflakes, any home that has little ones should be sure and make a dancing snowball arrangement. The kids love these, and they are so simple.
Combine: 2 T. baking soda
1 T. citric acid crystals
Put in a large glass brandy snifter or similar container.
Add: 2 lbs. mothballs (*not flakes*)
Fill with water.

The balls dance up and down and are so fun to watch. (Remember that moth-balls are very toxic, however, and so be careful to keep your little ones at a safe distance.)

Another fun idea for children is to build a little scene on a plastic tray with a foam base (don't use any metal). Put little branches, pine cones, little plastic houses, animals, or whatever you have. Glue everything in place. Then mix together:

    6 T. salt
    6 T. bluing
    6 T. water
    1 T. household ammonia

Mix well and carefully pour mixture over all the items in your scene that have *first* been moistened with water. Within a few hours "snowflakes" will start to form and will continue to grow for several days. These are so delicate and fragile looking — like a real fairyland. You'll have lots of fun playing around with this idea. Do be careful where you set your scene though, so it is out of the reach of tiny hands.

Now, when you are decorating for Christmas, no home is complete without a peach-pit kissing ball, a colonial tradition. Be sure and save your peach pits when you can peaches in the fall. Clean the pits well, cover a ball-shaped form with linoleum paste and start sticking the rounded end on with the pointed end sticking up. Start at the top and work down. Tie a large bow at the top, and hang it in a favorite doorway. Lots of fun and kisses will come your way.

When you are decorating with a natural theme, make some tapioca berries. They can be tucked into any arrangement or look pretty in a vase or container alone. To make them: Cut a three-inch piece of 21-gauge wire. Make a little fishhook loop on one end. Take a small ball of cotton and anchor it into the hook. Then roll the cotton ball in white glue and then in a dish of large "pearl" tapioca. With your fingers, shape the berry and hold the tapioca to the cotton ball until they hold securely. Make sure that the cotton ball is com-pletely covered. Let dry overnight. Then paint the berries with model or hobby paint in colors to resemble blackberries, rasp-berries, etc. These little things can add a touch of color to any dry arrangement.

Every front door needs an old-fashioned welcoming bell pull. These help your guests and family feel the festive air as they enter the house, and because they are so easy and inexpensive to make, you'll probably want to make several for gifts. To begin with, buy some jute chair webbing. Cut a twelve-inch length (or however long you want your bell pull to be). Now do a cross stitch (or any type of decorative stitch

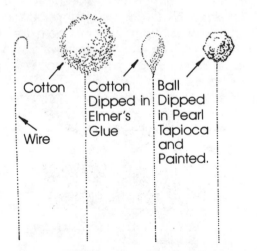

Cotton

Cotton Dipped in Elmer's Glue

Ball Dipped in Pearl Tapioca and Painted.

Wire

you prefer) design in yarn down the premarked border to cover the blue stripes. I then cut the letters spelling WELCOME out of felt to glue on down the strip of webbing. Miter the bottom edge of webbing to form a point and sew a bell at the end of the point. Turn under a hem at the top of the strip to form a casing to run a cord through for hanging, and you're all set. These can be varied in so many ways, and are so simple. Make a bunch up for your friends this year! Bells are usually cheaper on cards of six, anyway!

Rose Brandy Snifter Pattern

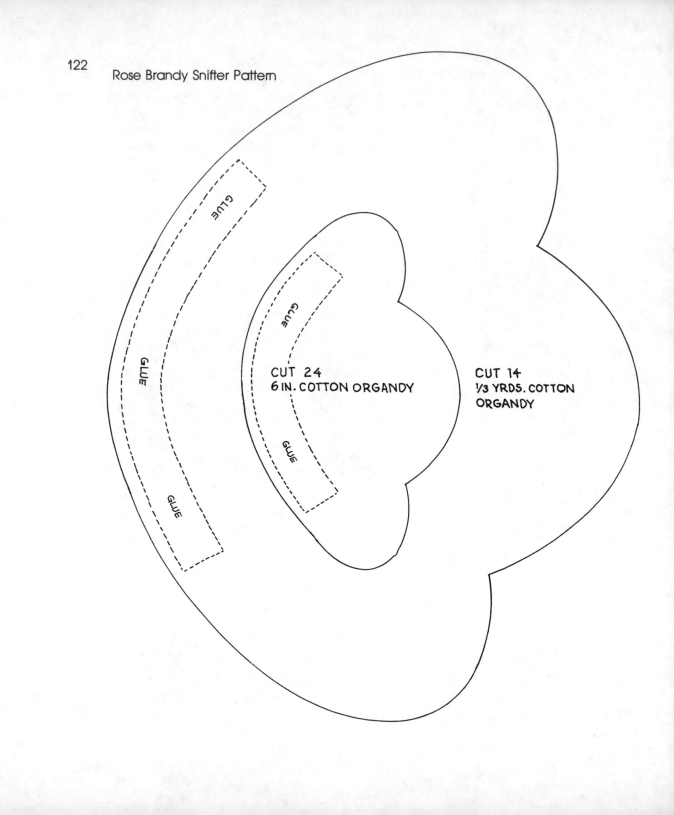

GLUE

GLUE

GLUE

GLUE

GLUE

GLUE

CUT 24
6 IN. COTTON ORGANDY

CUT 14
1/3 YRDS. COTTON ORGANDY

No dining-room table would be complete at Christmas without a pretty red rose candle holder. These are made from a medium-sized brandy snifter (with a four-inch mouth) and red *cotton* organdy. To make roses, cut out your petals, then roll the tops of each three sections over a toothpick to give them a slight curl. Begin gluing petals with white glue on the brandy snifter, starting at the top with the smaller petals, and work down. Have the petals extend a little beyond the top of the snifter but not so much that they will catch fire from the flame. When all the petals are on, cover the base of the snifter with green leaves. Make your own or buy velvety ones at the craft store (the type used for artificial flowers). Then put a little votive candle down in the snifter, and you have a beautiful centerpiece.

Once your home is all decorated and you are feeling the spirit of Christmas, it's time to share gifts with those we love. Nothing conveys our love more than gifts we have made with talents the Lord blessed us with. It is truly giving of ourselves and says, "I care."

I love to make pillowcases because you can personalize them in so many ways. For a standard pillow, cut a piece of fabric 14-x-33 inches. This will allow for a three inch hem and a side seam. Watch for nylon tricot on special. These make especially nice pillowcases. They will keep your hair from messing up so much while sleeping and also have a cool feeling on hot summer nights. To make these, you can eliminate the three-inch hem and just edge them with lace as we did our slips in Chapter 3.

It's also fun and economical to make

124 pillowcases from pretty printed sheets. You can get four pillowcases from one flat sheet and still have a strip to trim a plain white top sheet so that you have a matching ensemble. Use your fabric scraps to applique things on a plain pillowcase for a child. Learning aids, like numbers or letters, or items meaningful in their lives are especially good. How about a pillowcase with a pocket or two on the end for a pretty hanky, etc for someone that is bedridden?

We are a family of pillow lovers, and we have pillows all over the house by the bunches—on our window seats in the bay windows, on the couches, piled on the beds, and even pillows for the floor. (Those are a must for Mark and Roy to stretch out with!) Everyone loves pillows as a gift. Everything from fancy lacy ones to kneeling pillows for yard work are appreciated. If you are doing practical type pillows that will be used a lot and need laundering just be sure and stuff them with a dacron batting, polyester foam, or something washable.

Patchwork and applique pillows are fun to do. The scraps of lace and trim and pieces of ribbon you've been saving can be sewn patchwork style on a pastel background, such as a pillow top. Or try making some little pillows for the youngsters (even pillowcases) out of *flannel*. They love the cuddly warm feeling. You can buy pillow forms, but I use old bed pillows that have "seen their better days," or buy inexpensive bed pillows at the dime store and cut them in two; it's cheaper. Just remember, these pillows are for comfort, so don't make them too little or they are useless.

To make a nice gift for a gardener, save your old polyester knit scraps, shred them up, and stuff a pillow made of denim. Remember, this is the fabric that pine needles don't penetrate. Trim it with some iron-on tape in their name, a cute saying, or some flowers. It's a perfect "kneeling" pillow when working in the yard and can be laundered easily.

Another fun gift in the pillow area is this door—hanging pillow idea.

Nearly all the dime stores and craft shops carry the large wooden letters now. These make fun gifts—just finish them in any varnish or paint you choose and screw into them a doorstop (the metal kind with a rubber tip). They make great clothes hooks in the children's child's room, coat hooks in a hallway, or towel holders in a bathroom. Everyone loves them. If your husband is handy with a saw, he could even saw the letters out for you.

Since nothing makes a meal more special than hot rolls or muffins, why not make a cute little chicken bun warmer out of that quilted fabric you found on sale? You can even make some matching place mats. And if you're lucky to find matching unquilted fabric, make some napkins to go along, too. If you don't find the matching fabric, use a coordinating plain color. I discovered a really slick way to hem napkins. Since the commercial ones just have a zigzagged stitching on the edge, I do that, too. But, since it is almost impossible to zigzag along a cut edge, I take my whole big piece of fabric, draw out my squares for napkins, then stitch with a wide but close-together zigzag stitch all around each napkin. After I stitch, I cut them out with my little

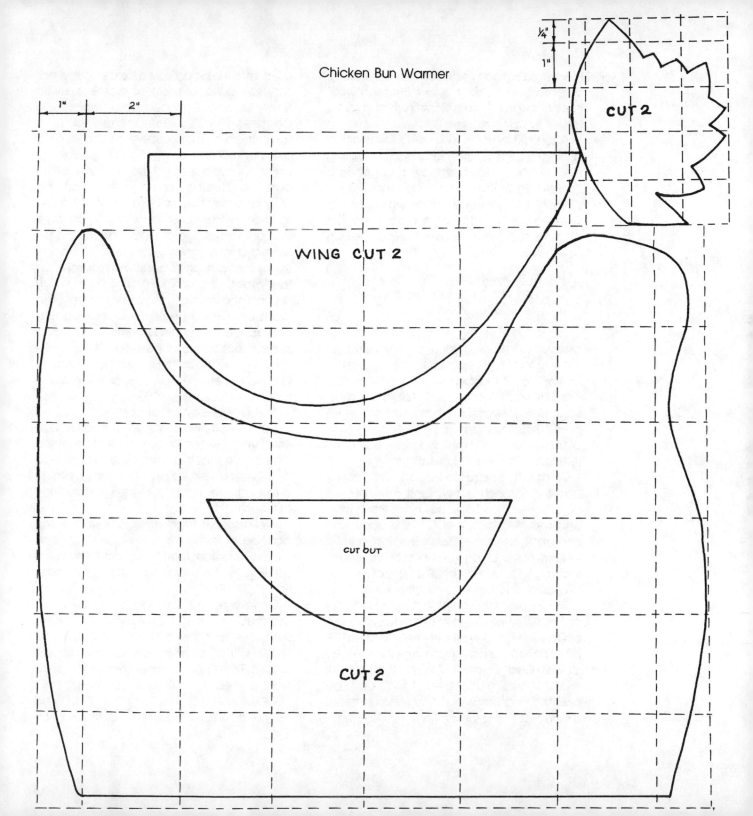

Chicken Bun Warmer

WING CUT 2

CUT 2

CUT OUT

CUT 2

manicure scissors *real* close to the stitching edge. You'll waste a little fabric this way, but it sure gives you a nicer finish and saves lots of frazzled nerves.

A fun gift that the kids will enjoy making and giving is to get some nice-smelling bars of soap with a smooth top. (White is preferable.) Then cut little squares of paper (either tissue or a white paper napkin separated) to fit the top of the bar of soap. Type messages on the paper such as —

This bar belongs to Billy Jones.
Did you wash behind the ears?
Bubble your troubles away.
Mr. Clean

or use your imagination. Lightly dampen the bar to stick the paper to it, then dip the entire top of the bar of soap into melted paraffin and let harden. Your little messages will last until the bar is just a sliver! A pretty little basket or box of these bars along with a pretty hand-trimmed towel (Chapter 7) make a great gift.

A much appreciated gift for father, uncle, or grandpa is a paintbrush-cleaner can. Save a large "juice" can, wash well, and remove the label. Nail the can in the center of a square board (being careful not to make a large hole that will cause leaking.) Cut a yardstick or narrow slat in two and nail the strips to the sides of the board so that they stick out to the sides of the can. Notch the tops of the two sticks so a little metal dowel can rest on them. A paintbrush can be hung from the metal dowel and suspended into the can. It really works neat. These, too, can be painted or decorated to personalize them.

Now Christmas is never complete with-out all the fun goodies we fix to eat. A great way to start off Christmas morning is with Sherry Jones's Orange Bubble Loaf. (See Chapter 9.) It's terrific served with scrambled eggs, sausage, and a big cold glass of milk.

For our main meal of the day, it's always easy to decide on a meat, but the accompaniments and salads are harder to choose. Here are a few of our favorites.

Cranberries or cranberry sauce can be served a very pretty way in fluted orange cups. Just cut an orange in half, remove the "meat," then with a paring knife, notch around the top of the orange peel. The cranberry-filled peels look nice sitting around the turkey and trimmings. You can serve sherbet in orange peels, too.

I like Jello salads for the holidays because they are always ready. A favorite is Snowball Christmas Surprise.

A really delicious accompaniment for Christmas dinner is Pioneer Pumpkin Muffins. Everyone raves about them, and the nice part is that they can be made ahead and frozen. Then warm them in the oven for a few minutes and everyone will think they are freshly baked.

We also like foods for the holidays that can be enjoyed as we sit and visit with friends. Our fondue is a good one, and I especially like it because it is nonalcoholic.

Quite a few of my baked goodies and candies are in my book, *A Family Raised on Sunshine*. But there are a couple more recipes that people are always asking about. They are so easy that a recipe is hardly needed, but boy! are they good.

One is our toasted coconut cups. This recipe came about from an experiment,

ZIPPY CARROTS AND GREEN BEANS

2 cups carrot strips
2 cups green beans
(cut or whole)
(Cook vegetables separately
until tender but not soft.)
Combine: 4 T. lemon juice
          2 T. salad oil

1/2 small onion,
chopped
2 celery stalks
chopped with leaves
1/4 tsp. basil
1/4 tsp. oregano
Salt and pepper to
taste.

Toss the cooked carrots and green beans in seasonings and store in a tightly covered container overnight. Turn the container several times. Serve cold as a relish.
Yum!

VIRGINIA ROWE'S CHRISTMAS CRANBERRY SALAD

(She's terrific and so is this salad!)
Dissolve: 1 3-ounce package cherry Jello in 1 cup hot water.
    Stir in: 3/4 cup sugar
            1 T. lemon juice
            3/4 cup pineapple juice
            1 cup ground cranberries
            1 ground orange (peel and all)
            1 cup drained crushed pineapple
            1 cup chopped celery
            1/2 cup chopped nuts

Stir occasionally as it is setting so that it is mixed well.
Serves 6.

SNOWBALL CHRISTMAS SURPRISE

Dissolve: 2 3-oz. packages cherry Jello in 2 cups hot water.

Add: 1 cup cold water
1 large package frozen strawberries.

Stir to thaw strawberries.
Form tiny balls (about the size of marbles) out of softened cream cheese and roll in finely chopped pecans. Put these around the bottom of your mold or bowl and pour partially set Jello mixture over.
Let set. Makes 8-10 servings.

PIONEER PUMPKIN MUFFINS

Cream: 1 1/4 cups sugar
1 stick margarine
1 1/2 cups canned pumpkin or cooked squash or sweet potatoes
Add: 3 eggs
Mix well.
Add: 1 cup milk
Then add: 1 3/4 cups flour
Dash of salt
1 1/2 tsp. cinnamon
1/2 tsp. nutmeg
2 tsp. baking powder
Fold in: 1/2 cup currants
1/2 cup chopped nuts (black walnuts are really good)

Bake in greased muffin tins at 400 degrees for about 25 minutes.

FUN FONDUE

Take 1/4 cup from one 7-oz. bottle of 7-Up (or carbonated lemon-lime beverage). Set aside. Pour the rest of the bottle into a heavy saucepan.

    Add: to saucepan 1 crushed garlic clove
    Bring to boil.
    Add: 1 lb. swiss cheese (cubed)

Stir until cheese melts. Then turn heat very low.

Combine: 1 1/2 T. flour
    1/4 cup 7-Up (saved from bottle)
    Add: 1/2 tsp. salt
    1/2 tsp. Worcestershire sauce

Stir into cheese mixture.
Cook and stir until smooth and thickened.
Serve in fondue dish with lightly toasted french bread cubes.

since Kristen and I love the commercial coconut cups so much. First, I toast a large cookie sheet full of shredded or flaked coconut in a 375 degree oven, stirring it often so that it browns nicely. Then I melt a couple of chunks of "chunk" or dipping chocolate. This is available in most grocery stores at holiday time. (If you want to stock up, it will keep well in a cool place.) *Don't* use chocolate chips. When the chocolate is melted (and be sure you use *real* low heat or a double boiler—hot temperatures make the chocolate get grainy. Be sure to stir it while it is melting) just dump in as much coconut as it will hold but still coat the coconut. Then drop by spoonsful into little candy cup papers and let harden.

Our other favorite is the same principle applied to Rice Krispies. Just stir as many Rice Krispies into the chocolate as will coat well. Then drop onto papers. Tastes just like the candy bars, and you get *lots* of candy for the amount of chocolate you use.

By the way, for a fun variety when making the traditional marshmallow-Rice Krispies bars, put in some chocolate chips instead of peanuts. Sure is good.

For a final pretty touch to your cakes,

especially fruitcake, roll out green gum-drops (like we did in Chapter 5 and in *A Family Raised on Sunshine* to make the roses) and cut holly-shaped leaves. Use little red hots for the berries. It looks so cute.

Though all the frills and goodies are fun, the true meaning of Christmas is in our hearts and attitudes and our joyful to-getherness at this holiday time. We all look forward to delivering the gingerbread houses and plates of cookies to our special friends, singing carols that express our happiness and thanksgiving, and spend-ing a few minutes at this busy time of year to see the joy in other families, too.

A feeling of calmness always comes over our home on Christmas Eve. After we have our usual chili supper, the kids light the tree and all our Christmas candles, and we gather around the fire with Roy in his favorite rocker. Each one has an opportu-nity to reflect on his blessings, and then Roy reads the Christmas story from the Book of Luke in our old family Bible. Then we have family prayer and gather around the piano while Kristen accompanies us to sing some carols. Heidi will sometimes join in on the flute, then we enjoy a plate of treats and milk. Of course, someone leaves a little plate under the tree for Santa. Our kids are nineteen, twenty-one, twenty-three, and twenty-four years old now, but our plate of cookies is still always there. They all hang their stockings and go off to bed. (Heidi made the stockings a few years ago when she was starting to sew and there are even two little ones for Roy and me that looked like Santa's socks. They were simply cut from different colors of felt and sewed together. Stephen has a lo-o-ong leg (boney knee and all) in a basketball sock

and shoe made from felt. Mark's is a maroon-and-white "Plano High" stocking.)

A decision is made when we go to bed about how early we'll get up. The first one awake at the agreed-upon hour wakes everyone else. Roy and I go down first and turn on the Christmas lights, and then the kids come down. We have done it this way since the kids were born. Then we gather 'round the tree and one person passes out the gifts one at a time so that we can all watch them being opened. It seems so much more meaningful this way, and we each have time to show our appreciation to one another. It's so fun to watch someone squeal for joy over a beautifully made gift and listen to the gift-giver tell some of the funny experiences that hap-pened while working on the gift. Some-times they are really touching experiences, and we all learn what true giving is all about.

Let's keep this beautiful Christmas spirit "growing" in our homes all year long and cultivate it with all the tender loving care it deserves.

9

Tradition
Tradition

When Heidi was a little girl, her most frequently asked question was, "When are we going to get there?" no matter if it were a trip to Utah or to the grocery store. Too often we live our lives like that—thinking we will reach our destination of happiness at some later time. We forget that life is a journey and not a destination. Many, many times as I was growing up, I remember Mom counseling me not to wish my life away. Soon I had a little family of my own and could see the wisdom in her words. Each day should be special, and it can be if we make it that way. It's so sad to see someone work hard toward something only to reach it and realize that life has passed him by. Living happily, usefully, and lovingly is the most important part of "getting there."

One of my favorite quotes is from Horace. "Whatever hour God has blessed you with, take it with grateful hand; nor postpone your joys from year to year, so that in whatever place you have been, you may say that you have lived happily." As homemakers, we have the ability to instil this in our husbands and children, as well as ourselves, by doing the "little things" that make days memorable and by establishing traditions.

As I visit with friends and neighbors, they usually say, "Oh, we don't have many traditions." But, have you ever stopped to think just how many habits and expected routines you establish in your day-to-day living? Would everyone be shocked if Dad got up in the morning before Mom (or vice versa), or if Mark didn't lick the bowl after Mom made cookies, because this is the way it "always" is? That's tradition. It helps build self-worth and gives a sense of continuity and belonging—a feeling that is greatly needed in our world today. We don't always realize the full impact of these little things until our grown children return home and comment on the good feeling these traditions give them.

Traditions are also that link with the past that helps preserve our heritage. Many of the lasting values of life are learned this way; such as the sharing and showing of affection by the Polish people. At Christmastime, gathered around the table, they give each other a bite of their wafer, embrace and express their love. The Maori people of New Zealand express their traditions in their legends, songs, stories, and dances. Whether your ancestors were German, Irish, American Indian, or Japanese; whether your family lives in the South, the Midwest, or New England; your own unique heritage can be preserved in your family's traditions.

Roy and I had many long talks before we were married about our goals and expectations of marriage and raising a family, so we set up some guidelines right then. Of course, these constantly change and grow as our lives progress. For you young people, I heartily recommend starting this way. It's like building your house on a rock foundation instead of sand. On the other hand, it's never too late to set new goals and ideals. After all, ten years from now you'll be ten years older no matter what, so you might as well start now to make those years happier.

The first tradition we started in our home was to never go to bed mad, and to always kneel in prayer together before we went to bed. Some nights we had to stay up kinda late working something out, but

134 we always stuck with it. I like this tradition because then we always go to bed *together*. I may nap on the couch while he's finishing up a project or attending a meeting, or Roy may stretch out on the floor (he loves that!) while I'm doing the last of the ironing, but then we are off to bed together.

As our kids have joined our family, we have continued to have family prayer, kneeling around our bed at night and around the breakfast table in the morning. Everyone takes turns, and this has brought so much closeness to our family. Sunday dinner is *always* Dad's turn, though; that's tradition, too!

Roy has always helped me to be seated at the table, and through this and many other kindnesses he has established tradition with our boys, who now do the same. Traditions give a family a sense of security. Children thrive on this and will be the first to remind you when you forget.

Traditions can also help you run a more orderly household. The kids always looked forward to bath-time, and they had great fun, but at first the big clutter of bath toys made a big mess. We soon established another tradition, "three toys only in the tub." Our bathroom always had a fishnet hanging above the tub. We put two hooks on the wall above the tub about four feet apart and bought an inexpensive fishnet at an import store. Then the net was hung from the hooks. The wet toys could be tossed into it as it hung in "hammock" style, and any excess water just dripped into the tub. It sure saved a lot of headaches. (Have you ever tried getting *all* of the water out of a doll's head, and then *still* found puddles on the closet floor?)

Establishing a bedtime is a tradition that can be a big help to everyone. Several of my kids' schoolteachers have told me they can always tell the children that have set bedtimes. They are brighter and more alert, as well as being more *self-disciplined*. Family rules and guidelines sure help develop this. A regular, *disciplined bedtime* was established in our family council meeting and adhered to faithfully. I think it really takes more discipline on the part of a parent than the child. But it pays off in so many ways. The children respect you more, they feel they are genuinely cared about, and they feel so much better physically for having an established sleeping pattern. As a parent, first show them lots of love, explain the reasoning for an established bedtime, make sure they are comfortable and have all necessary things taken care of (like a drink of water), firmly say goodnight and express your love again. Then comes the most important ingredient—be consistent. It takes effort on your part, but I can't begin to tell you the benefits you will share.

Little ones—and grown ups, too—don't always want to go to bed when they should, but that doesn't mean bedtime can't be fun. All children love stories, and it gives parents a chance to exhibit the "ham" in them. As you read or tell stories to your family, don't be afraid to embellish them with sound effects or actions. It can be very relaxing for a parent at the end of the day to "loosen up" and really get into the story. Try it, it really works. A story becomes a lot more real and exciting when the duck is "quacking," the fire truck siren "blares" down the street or the birds are "cheeping, chattering, and fluttering their wings." Our favorite story had a character with a strong southern accent, and the kids just loved it when I would do that particular one. After a fun storytelling experience, I guarantee you both a good night's sleep.

To let each child know how much he is cared about, why not let Daddy spend one bedtime a week for a little private "conference talk." A father can feel left out since we as mothers get to share so many things with our children while husbands are away, and children need a good relationship with their fathers, too. Roy made it a practice of taking each girl out to eat occasionally for a Saturday breakfast (Kristen really loved those special times at the pancake house) or a Friday night hamburger. Often he would take just one boy to play golf or go fishing. I know they had some choice conversations at times like this, and they always will be special memories, too.

As our children grew, we established set times for other activities, such as homework. And along with set times, we provided our young scholars with a comfortable and workable area with good lighting for study. This doesn't have to be expensive. We got a big old library table for the boys from a junk store for a couple of dollars. We then worked together to refinish it, and it was a perfect study table. (Now that the boys are gone, we cut the legs down, and have the neatest coffee table. It's such a heavy and sturdy piece, we eat snacks around it, play games on it, rest our feet on it, etc., and we sure have gotten our two dollars' worth! A good coat of wax now and then, and it will last forever.) Anyway, back to study areas, we picked up a little

desk for the girls from a hotel that was changing some furniture. It was free; we just had to pick it up. That little desk was painted several different colors and trims while we had it to go with their room decor. It has now been passed on to another young family. The point is to provide everyone with a study area of his or her own if possible. We also found it was much more conducive to study if we all were reading, writing, or studying. Especially when the kids were little, it was hard to expect them to be upstairs studying if everyone else was downstairs laughing at something on the TV. It didn't take us long to discover that the TV didn't *have* to be on all of the time. Roy and I could use the time to good advantage, too, by reading or doing some letter writing. So, we all benefitted. Like I said before, "it's lots more fun to work or play if someone is doing it with you."

One of our mottos was "many hands make light work." If it were Steve's turn to mow the yard, and Mark had finished his job already, Mark knew they could play ball together sooner if he helped, so off he ran to get the rake.

In the summer we had such a good time doing our canning and freezing. The kids would sit in a big circle out in the yard and husk corn or whatever. Soon half of the neighbor kids wanted to help. The two keys to success here are (1) work *with* them, and (2) make it fun. Joke about things, have contests, or play word games while working. The chore has to be done anyway. Attitude turns work into play. Then, let them share in the satisfaction of a job well done. Let them show Daddy all those nice bags of corn in the freezer when he gets home.

KRAUT RUNZAS

Prepare any yeast roll or bread dough. Let rise.
Brown: 1 lb. ground beef
  Add: 1 cup finely grated cabbage
        1 tsp. caraway seed
        Salt & pepper to taste
Cook until cabbage is tender.
Roll dough out thin (about 1/4 inch thick). Cut in 4-inch squares or circles. Put a heaping spoonful of meat on half of square. Fold over other half and pinch squares together. Let set on greased cookie sheet about 10-15 minutes.
Bake at 350 degrees for 30-40 minutes.
Serve with chili sauce.

LAURIA'S PIZZA DOUGH

Dissolve 2 pkgs. yeast in 1/2 cup warm water.
Put 4 cups flour in bowl — make a well in center.

Add: 1/4 cup oil
1 tsp. salt
1 cup warm water
Yeast mixture

Knead well on floured board.
Cover. Let rise until double.
Roll out two 14-inch pizzas on oiled pans. Spread each with 1/2 small can tomato sauce.
Sprinkle with: garlic   sweet basil
                    oregano   minced onion
Top with meat as desired. (We like pepperoni or sausage — crumbled and browned.)
Cover with grated cheese. A mixture of mozzarella or swiss and cheddar is good.
Let rise again. Bake at 425 degrees until done.

PITA BREAD (for gyros)

Dissolve: 1 pkg. dry yeast in 1 1/4 cups warm water.
Add: 2 tsp. sugar
Then add: 1 tsp. salt
2 T. oil
2 cups flour

Beat well with mixer for 3 minutes.
Add: 1 1/2 cups flour
Knead on floured board about 5 minutes.
Cover and let rise for 30 minutes.

Divide into 10 or 12 balls. Roll out into 5-6 inch circles. Always roll from the middle out or you will have bubbles puffing up.
Put on ungreased cookie sheet.
Brush with evaporated milk.
Let rise about 1/2 hour or until light.
Bake at 400 degrees for about 10-15 minutes — until nicely browned.
Cool on rack.
To serve, slit bread along one side to form a pocket. Stuff with filling.

Speaking of things in the freezer, we always have our own "convenience" section in ours. That way, we don't have to pay the horrible prices for these at the grocery store or run to a fast food place when we need to eat in a hurry. It's so much fun to sit around the kitchen table and make up things "assembly-line style." Pop them in the freezer, and your own convenience foods are ready to eat at the drop of a hat. Several of our good recipes for this idea are in *A Family Raised On Sunshine.* But here are some more of our favorites. We especially like these because they each have an ethnic background, and give us a taste of another culture.

Keep some of each of these things in your freezer, and you'll be a big hit with everyone.

One family night when we were having

FILLING

In fry pan heat 3 T. oil.
Brown: 2 lbs. beef (I use round
         steak cut in thin strips).

When well browned, add:
       2 stalks celery with leaves (diced)
       1 onion, diced
       1 small eggplant (peeled and diced)
       1/2 tsp. garlic salt
       pepper
       1 cup chili sauce
       3 chopped tomatoes or 1 1-lb. can of tomatoes.
Let simmer 1 hour.
Spoon into pitas and top with sour cream, shredded cheese, and black olives.
To freeze, freeze pita bread in bags and the filling in a separate container.
Ooh! are they delicious!

a meeting, our kids gave me an insight into getting things done. They said they didn't mind doing the chores, but they all agreed that they disliked coming into the house from school only to be met by "orders" of work to be done. So we all decided that the best way was for me to make little lists of each of their chores for the day and leave the list on their beds. Then, they could change their clothes, do the jobs on the list, and leave the completed list on the kitchen table when they were finished. We were all surprised at how smoothly this worked. Soon we had a list by the week. Everyone had a sense of accomplishment, and no harsh words were spoken. Sometimes I even put one or two fun things on their lists like have milk and cookies with

Mom or treat your friend to an ice cream cone, just to add a little spice.

Those lists have become such a tradition at our house that Roy and I still use them.

When we sat down with our family recently and asked them which traditions they remember most, our youngest, Heidi, piped up with "We got to start wearing a little makeup when we were thirteen." We have found that by establishing traditions like this, the kids really looked forward to these events, and it becomes more meaningful. Some others were group parties at age fourteen, no single dating until age sixteen. These were exciting milestones in their lives, and they knew we cared.

The tradition our boys laughed about was the family haircuts. Every two or three weeks, I set up a barber shop in the garage and cut their hair. (As soon as Roy and I were married, we saved our pennies and bought a set of clippers out of necessity!) The kids and Roy never went to a barber. All the neighbor kids in Kansas City would gather round, and we had a great time telling stories just like in the "old days." The boys still laugh about those "burr" cuts, but in time I got to be a pro—no nicks or anything. Roy still prefers my haircuts, so we have our regular barber sessions. I think he just likes the pampering. Don't be afraid to try haircuts on your family. Start first with little trims around the neck, or the ears, a few times until you get the feel of it. A good sharp scissors (barber scissors are best) and comb is all you need. Work at this until you feel comfortable then gradually increase working with the complete head. Take your time, though; don't try giving a complete haircut the first time, or you may end up with the "bowl on the head" look and you won't want to try again. It sure is a saver once you get the hang of it.

Another fun thing that was always going on at our house was our pixie game. On Monday nights at Family Home Evening, we drew names (the kids always got a kick out of this). Then you were a pixie all week for the person who's name you had drawn. No one was ever supposed to find out who his or her pixie was. Then the next Monday night, we'd all try to guess. It was so much fun to sneak in and turn that person's bed down at night, pin an "I love you" to his or her pillow, empty the garbage when it was his turn, drop a stick of gum into his lunch sack for a surprise, or put a little note or treat in his mail pocket (see Chapter 1). Why don't you try the pixie game at your house?

I have mentioned our family nights to you several times. Let me tell you a little about them. We really have our church (Mormon) to thank for them. It is a program where every family in the Mormon church designates Monday night as a time when nothing outside the family is planned. No meetings or other commitments are made, and the time is especially for the family. I always try to have an extra special supper. Then we all gather round, Dad presides, and we begin with family prayer and usually sing a song together. The song could be anything from a hymn to "You Are My Sunshine." We take turns planning the evening. It may be a scriptural lesson, a night ice skating, playing Monopoly, working on scrapbooks, or someone may have an important item to discuss. We close the evening with refreshments, and we also take turns with this. We used to have so much fun watching the kids prepare when it was one of their turns. They would shut the kitchen door and really work to make a super surprise! The evening is always ended with prayer. Sometimes we spend all evening for family night and other times we just spend an hour or so. I can sure tell you there is nothing like it to help your family grow together in love and understanding. Try it at your house.

All of us play some type of musical instrument, so many times we would spend an evening with our own concert. I would really recommend you save your pennies to invest in this area. Learning to play an instrument or develop an art is one of the most beautiful ways to develop a sense of self-worth and self-discipline. It also teaches the rest of the family patience! We'll never forget the "squeeking" coming from Kristen's room as she worked on her violin or Steve's beating on his drums. I was kinda glad when he switched to the tympani because then he had to practice at school! We got a double dose of patience, too, because Roy taught piano lessons at our house from 5:30 until 9:00 every week night for a while to help out

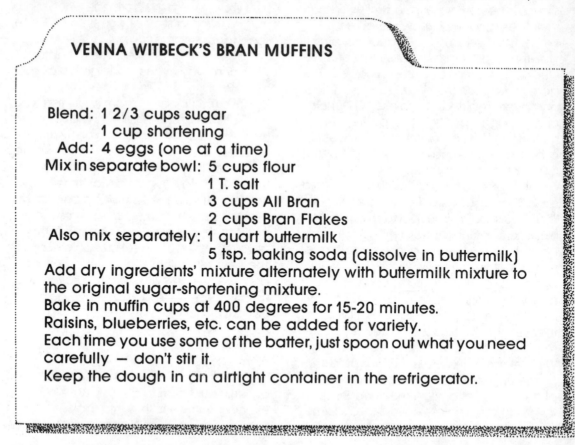

VENNA WITBECK'S BRAN MUFFINS

Blend: 1 2/3 cups sugar
       1 cup shortening
Add: 4 eggs (one at a time)
Mix in separate bowl: 5 cups flour
       1 T. salt
       3 cups All Bran
       2 cups Bran Flakes
Also mix separately: 1 quart buttermilk
       5 tsp. baking soda (dissolve in buttermilk)
Add dry ingredients' mixture alternately with buttermilk mixture to the original sugar-shortening mixture.
Bake in muffin cups at 400 degrees for 15-20 minutes.
Raisins, blueberries, etc. can be added for variety.
Each time you use some of the batter, just spoon out what you need carefully — don't stir it.
Keep the dough in an airtight container in the refrigerator.

financially. By the time our kids went in to have their lessons, they knew the song by heart from hearing it from so many students.

We also established the tradition of eating breakfast together. Even if it meant that someone had to get up a little earlier, we did. Then we used that extra time to study or practice a lesson. All of my family loves a big breakfast, so I think this muffin recipe has been one of my life-savers.

There are several variations of this being passed around and shared around the country, but if the recipe is new to you, give it a try. The batter keeps up to six weeks in the fridge, so you can bake a few at a time. I got this one from a dear friend in Kansas City.

Since we're talking about traditional recipes, I have to share my two daughters' favorites. We don't even have to ask them what they would like. This is *traditional!*

HEIDI'S LOUISIANA PORK CHOPS

Mix: in large fry pan 2 T. honey
1 tsp. Kitchen Bouquet
Bring to a simmer.
Brown 4 pork chops in this
mixture.

Take the browned pork chops out of the pan for a minute and add 1/2 cup apple cider (I like cider instead of juice; it's not as refined). Stir well and loosen all the little crispies.
Add: 4 yams (peeled and sliced)
4 apples (sliced but I don't peel them)
Put the pork chops back on top and sprinkle with:
1 1/2 tsp. salt
Dash of pepper
A little nutmeg and cinnamon
Bring the mixture to a boil, turn the heat way down, and cook slowly for about 1 hour. If necessary you can add a little more cider or apple juice.

KRISTEN'S DRIED BEEF CASSEROLE

Melt: 1/4 cup margarine in fry
pan.
Add: 1 pkg. or small glass of
dried beef (torn up into
little pieces)

Fry until frizzled.
Remove beef from pan and add:
1/2 tsp. salt
Dash of pepper
1/2 cup chopped onion
4 cups cubed potatoes
Cook for 3-4 minutes in the margarine.
Add: 1 cup boiling water
1 13-oz. can evaporated milk
Cook 30 minutes over low heat until potatoes are tender.
Add: Dried beef
1 T. parsley flakes
Cook for 5-10 minutes and serve. Serves 4-6.

Kristen has to have lots of fresh bread with her casserole so she can slick up the saucy gravy.

I guess if there is one special traditional recipe with the Nyes, it is Mandarin Orange Salad. I think I've given this recipe to more people than any other. It's a must at our house if there is company coming (or for *any* excuse we can find!).

The beauty of this recipe is that you can vary the flavor of Jello and types of fruit and really be inventive. I guarantee you'll love this one!

I hope you are baking your own bread now. Everyone loves warm freshly baked bread. When my bread comes out of the oven, one loaf is automatically wrapped in one of my bright cotton-print napkins

MANDARIN ORANGE SALAD

Prepare 2 3-oz. pkgs. orange Jello as directed in a 9x12 inch glass pan. When partially set, add:

  1 11-oz. can drained mandarin oranges
  1 16-oz. can drained crushed pineapple (retain juice from both fruits for the topping)
  2 bananas
  8-9 chopped maraschino cherries
  2 cups miniature marshmallows

Stir and let set.

TOPPING

 Mix: 1 egg
  2 T. flour
  1/2 cup sugar
  1 cup juice (combined mandarin orange juice and pine-apple juice saved from adding fruit to Jello)

Cook until thick.
Cool thoroughly.
Whip 1 cup whipping cream and fold into cold sauce.
Spread on top of Jello and sprinkle with grated cheddar cheese.
Makes 12 nice squares.

and taken to a friend or neighbor. It makes the bread taste twice as good to us.

If you'd like to make a hot bread to surprise your family but are rushed for time, here are two great ones to try using canned refrigerator biscuits.

You would *never* know that you used *canned* biscuits! It's delicious!

Roy and I have started a new tradition now. For our twenty-fifth anniversary, we went to Williamsburg, Virginia, and thoroughly enjoyed all of the beautiful antiques, history, and of course the delicious early American food. The Peanut Soup was the most unusual. We were skeptical at first, but since it is traditionally colonial,

SHERRY JONES'S ORANGE BUBBLE LOAF

Melt: 1 stick margarine
Add: 1 cup sugar
      1 orange rind (finely grated)

Take 3 cans refrigerator biscuits and separate each biscuit.
Dip each biscuit in the orange-butter mixture.
Stand each one on end in a circle in a bundt pan.
Complete filling the pan and use all biscuits.
Bake at 350 degrees for 30-40 minutes.
Turn out on platter and serve hot.

PIZZA BUBBLES

Preheat oven to 400 degrees.
    Melt: 1 T. margarine in round cake pan. Be sure it covers the bottom.

Mix together:
1/2 cup tomato sauce
1 T. oil
1/2 tsp. basil
1/2 tsp. oregano
1 clove garlic, minced
1/2 small chopped onion

Separate 1 can refrigerator biscuits (10). Cut each biscuit in 4 pieces.
Toss biscuit pieces in sauce and place in buttered pan.
Pour remaining sauce over and cover the top with 1/3 cup shredded cheese (mozzarella is best).
Bake at 400 degrees for about 20 minutes. Serve warm.

PEANUT SOUP

Sauté: (until soft but not brown)
      1 medium onion, chopped
      3 stalks celery, chopped
      1/4 cup margarine
  Stir: in 4 T. flour until well mixed.
  Add: 2 quarts chicken stock, stirring constantly.
      Bring to a boil. Remove from heat and strain.
  Add: 2 cups smooth peanut butter
      2 cups light cream
Blend thoroughly. Return to low heat and warm through.

OHIO BUCKEYES

Knead together: 1 1/2 cups chunky peanut butter
               1 1/2 lbs. powdered sugar
               2 sticks margarine
               1 1/2 tsp. vanilla

Shape into small balls.
Melt several pieces of chunk chocolate (this is the cut-up chunks of chocolate sold in grocery stores to be used for dipping) over hot water.
Stick a toothpick into each ball and dip into chocolate, leaving a circle on top uncoated to resemble a buckeye.
Set on waxed paper and chill to harden.
Can also be frozen.
Start a new tradition with your family today!

146   we had to try it. We have decided now to
       have it each anniversary, at least!

       We have continued to add traditions
       with our family as the years pass. We hope
       they will carry them on in their families for
       fun and colorful years to come.

       Since we are now living in Ohio, the
       Buckeye State, we have a dish of buck-
       eyes (or lucky beans my boys call them)
       sitting out. When we have out-of-state
       visitors, they are always invited to put one
       in their pocket to take home. I can't give
       each of you a buckeye, but I'll share with
       you a delicious candy called "Buckeyes"
       in honor of our state.

10

Your Own Special Rainbow:

Keeping It Bright

You are a unique person. Nobody else has the same combination of abilities and talents that you do. You have a gift that no one else has; you can bring joy and happiness in your own special way.

We are all different, and we shouldn't expect to talk alike, look alike, or excel in the same things as someone else. Let's be proud of our uniqueness.

We are all special children to our Heavenly Father, and as the scriptures tell us, if He cares about a fallen sparrow, how much more does He care about each one of us.

Are you keeping a personal journal to record all the happy, sad, and exciting things that are happening in your life? A written journal can be so rewarding and helpful. Not only will it help you grow as you look back and contemplate your life, but think of the value it will be to future generations to know and understand you. As your children and grandchildren read about your special days or learning experiences, it will be a great teacher and tool for them in their lives. Not all of us are fortunate enough to have our grandparents and great-grandparents around to give us the benefit of their learning, and how nice it is if these things are recorded for us to gain from. Reading their histories, we become better acquainted with them, gain a sense of belonging, and develop some insights into ourselves and our own behavior.

You don't have to be a literary genius. Just keep a book and pen by your bed, and every day or so, jot down thoughts or happenings. Those thoughts are *so* important. Many of us are a little shy to express our thoughts, but get them down on paper.

Great things are born this way.

Be sure and write things down *as they happen*. Time has a way of fading memories, and the most choice thing could be left out. It only takes a few minutes to record thoughts and happenings if you do it at the time.

Don't worry about your words having great meaning to the whole world. If they help you, a daughter or grandson to capture the feeling of a special moment or the faith or strength they need for a particular situation your thought will have achieved your purpose and goal.

Don't feel that these pages should be all typed up like a book. Nothing is more personal or meaningful than a person's handwriting. This is something worth preserving in its own right.

Be sure in your personal history that you also record medical data. Keep track of diseases and illnesses, shots, medication, height, weight at different ages, and any surgeries, eyeglass changes, etc. This can be a big help to you and valuable to your posterity.

As we keep our records, pictures play an important part. Color pictures fade with time and are not nearly as practical for keeping as black and white. Be sure to write the dates and names of people on the backs of pictures. At the time, we think we'll always remember, but I have already found myself in a position of wondering who someone was in a photograph from my childhood. I'm sure I thought I would never forget!

As you take pictures for your remembrance books, take "shots" of people in realistic surroundings and natural action, never stiff poses. Include meaningful background and be sure you are close enough to your subject so that they will be easily recognizable. These things make pictures so much more meaningful.

One of the most precious gifts we have ever received was for Christmas in 1977 when my sister, Donna, gave us a beautiful family history complete with portraits and snapshots of parents and grandparents back several generations, as well as personal stories of each of their lives. She spent all year collecting the photos and gathering information from friends and relatives. These special photos not only show us what our ancestors looked like, but their personalities show through in their expressions (remember that!) and it's fun to see the styles of clothes, hair, architecture, landscaping, and even glimpses of the customs of the time.

The tears run down my cheeks as I read about my father who died when I was two months old. I feel close to him as I read how "he helped his mother during canning season by washing jars in a tub of water outside, then shaking water and sand in them until they were clean." He was a real tease with his sister and a clown at milking time when the cats would line up so he could squirt milk into their mouths. His sense of humor kept things lively, also, while they did the butchering, making mettwurst (his favorite) and all the tempting sausages. When he was nineteen, he ordered a cheap violin through the catalog and taught himself to play. He soon mastered it and was working on a fifty-year-old second-hand piano with his sister. Before long they had a small orchestra in demand to play for dances. He even had the privilege of playing with Lawrence Welk.

Kristen and I love to read the sections about my mother because Kristen is so much like her. They are both a little on the quiet, shy side but very compassionate and sensitive to people's feelings; and also very creative in music and crafts such as sewing and decorating. Mom was a milliner in her early life and created beautiful hats. Kristen was also designing things for her dolls before she started school. They both also enjoy the piano.

Now Heidi and I have discovered she is the spittin' image of Grandma Scheel, a real go-getter.

Grandma Scheel came from Schleswig-Schlho-Prussia, Germany. A bride at age sixteen in Nebraska, she made beautiful furniture for their humble house including kitchen cupboards, a straw mattress (a favorite of her husband), and a long bench for the children to sit on while they ate. She even created different effects in her furniture's finish by using a metal comb and other objects.

Baking was another of her talents, and she was noted for her whole wheat bread, biscuits, and cookies. She had a ten-gallon crock filled with her cookies hidden under the stairway, but the grandchildren always knew where to find it.

Many parties and celebrations were held at their farm, and it was common for her to prepare a big ham to slice, potato salad, salmon salad, and goodies including twenty cakes, all for one event. (All her cooking was done on a wood-burning stove.) She even fashioned a cold storage well under the floor of the porch. Things kept down in this well were always refreshingly cool. She enjoyed working in her garden and never sat down to rest unless she was patching overalls or darning stockings. She liked to sew and made all her own and family's clothing.

Now, Grandma Benson was a "go-getter" in her own right. She loved to perform on the stage and never missed an opportunity to volunteer her talents or those of her children or grandchildren. She loved people and doing things for and with them. She also was very style conscious and did a lot of dress designing. I don't think she ever wore an outfit the same way twice. She always varied it by changing a collar, cuffs, or trim. She was also very practical and delighted in making an outfit out of "nothing."

We treasure the memories of ancestors. Our oldest son, Stephen, was thrilled when he was privileged to serve his two-year mission for the church in Germany and actually walk the streets where these people had walked and lived. He also became fluent in their language. That is my next goal. I want to learn a foreign language, and German seems the logical one. I purchased a record set for under ten dollars and am working on it in my spare time. Steve chuckles at me and my pronunciations sometimes, but I'll make it. As I said in Chapter 2, we should be learning and growing always.

Learning a foreign language is beneficial in so many ways. It teaches us self-discipline (which we all need more of), it helps bridge a gap between us and another part of the world, and provides us with a better mastery of our own language.

In addition to keeping a personal history in word and picture form, it is so meaningful to keep a pedigree chart of your family. It is so interesting as well as helpful to have a record of your ancestors. The Mormon church has printed sheets you can use for this that are simple to fill out. You can obtain copies of these sheets from the Genealogical Society, 50 East North Temple, Salt Lake City, UT 84150. Just write and request a price list and order forms.

It's so fun to gather the information to fill out your pedigree chart. Write letters to living relatives or, better yet, take your little cassette recorder and go spend an afternoon with them. You'll hear stories that you'll always remember and treasure. Walking through an old cemetery checking tombstones can be a real learning experience for the whole family. Family vacations can be built around a part of the country where you can learn of relatives. County records such as probate, land, court, and vital statistics have valuable information. The address above can provide you with both printed material for sources of reference and also addresses in your area of genealogical libraries. Census records can also be checked. Public libraries, newspaper offices, and many areas even have local genealogical libraries available to the public. So often as our relatives pass away, their photographs, clippings, and papers are burned or discarded. Don't let this happen in your family. Help this person and his valuable life live forever.

Even though you are keeping a personal journal and scrapbook, there are always other items that don't fall into either catagory. Like your favorite stuffed toy from childhood, a little trophy you won in your first contest, or that precious "hand" plaque your young daughter gave you for Mother's Day. We have created what we call at our house a *keepsake box* for each of us. Mine is full of little treasures that I hope someday will help someone to know me a little better. We also started one for each of our children when they were born. As they outgrew a favorite toy or special little outfit, it was carefully cleaned, wrapped in tissue, and placed in their keepsake box. We have had some very special family nights when we sat together and went through our boxes, sharing happy and sad memories with one another. One item like Steve's little Huckleberry Hound watch brought a flood of memories back to all of us of his closeness to dying and stay in the hospital with a severe concussion and his delight to watch the minutes tick by on his new watch. Things become very real again.

Get your family together soon, and make a keepsake box for each member. Just make sure they are good, sturdy boxes. We all put different values on things and wish to save what *we* think is special. I always smile when I see the little beat-up, black rubber wheel that the boys neatly wrapped away. But to them it means a great deal. They spent hours together playing with that old wheel, creating new games and challenges.

What a choice gift we will be giving our children if we help them develop creativity and have respect for themselves and others. If they grow up with these things, they will be able to cope with the stresses and strains of today's world. Raising children is like holding a bar of slippery soap. If you hold it too tightly, it spurts from your hand; if you hold it too loosely, it slips away. With a gentle but firm hand your children will stay close to you and follow your lead.

We as mothers have the greatest opportunity to help our youngsters have a good self-image. More than anyone else, we build in them the feelings they have of themselves. The comments we make to them or about them shape their opinions of themselves. Do we say, "I've never seen such a picky eater," "Why don't you eat what's on your plate like Johnny does," or "I just hate to cook for you"? If he is getting all this attention for these habits, will he want to change? Will he think he has the ability to change? If they hear us say, "He has the worst temper I've ever seen," "He is always doing something wrong," or "He drives me crazy," will they want to try to be better? If he hears himself called "clumsy" over and over, will he begin to *expect* himself to be awkward and ill-at-ease? Children, being so impressionable, are especially likely to live up to what we think of them. Think what an exciting challenge that is. As mothers, we can help form these little ones into very choice and special spirits with kind remarks and sincere compliments.

Nothing that you give your husband and children will ever be as important as a sense of self worth and the knowledge that they are a special individual.

One of my most treasured items in my keepsake box — a letter from my son, Mark, when he was away on his mission for the church — points out this principle very strongly to me:

"I've been thinking about you all morning.... So I thought I would write you a short note to tell you how much I love you and miss you. The patience you've had with me and the faith you've shown in me, mean the world. You've always shown your confidence in me and spurred me on to do something I didn't think I could do. You've always helped me gather courage and strength in all that I've done. I don't think I could have accomplished anything I have done so far in my life without your love, faith, and encouragement. I have always tried to do my best in what I have done because I knew that you knew I could. — I love you. You have trained me and taught me so well in the Gospel and how to be happy. I don't think I can ever repay you. Life is beautiful, and you have made it that way...."

A priceless treasure in my keepsake box! I hope you don't mind my sharing this with you, but mothers, the opportunities we have in raising our families are limitless. Give it your all.

We have to set good examples for our families. Being a mother is more than a biological process. It is a life of love, patience, sacrifice, and *teaching* by example. Since none of us are perfect, we can help our children understand the principle of repentance and patience. This way we grow together and share *respect*. That little word is so important. We hear so much about children respecting their parents, but do we as parents respect our children as individuals, also? True, we need to train, guide, and direct them, but always in love and respect for them as children of God. Children need discipline and guidelines, or life would be like streets without traffic lights. But help them to understand the rules and consequences, or you will have a child that feels hurt, puzzled, or rejected. If the child realizes you disapprove of what he has done but still love him very much, he will try much harder not to repeat his mistake.

I am always troubled when I hear a mother say, "I won't be bothered helping him on a project because I'm just too busy right now and besides, he should have planned better." Heavens, many times I've had to rely on the help of my husband or children to do a project, and I would have been in a mess if they had that attitude. We are all human and need others. Life is a give-and-take situation, and this is what family life is all about.

One of my favorite poems is by Mildred Howell —

A little seed lay in the ground
and soon began to sprout.
"Now which of the flowers all around,"
it mused, "shall I come out?"
"The lily's face is fair and proud,
but just a trifle cold;
the rose, I think is rather loud,
and then its fashion's old.
The violet is very well,
but not a flower I'd choose;
nor yet the canterbury bell,
I never cared for blues.
Petunias are by far too bright
and common flowers besides;
the primrose only blooms at night,
and peonies spread too wide."
And so it criticized each flower,
this supercilious seed;
until it woke one summer hour,
and found itself a weed.

There is a profound lesson here. When we're forever grumbling and nothing looks right but ourselves, we can easily turn into a weed. If we look for the good in others, we both grow.

We all have faults, but we need to be

154 accepted in spite of our shortcomings, and we need to be seen through eyes that are kind and merciful. If we desire to live in a home of kindness and one that is free from unkind criticism, it must begin with us.

In building self-worth and family unity, we have found one of the biggest motivators is our family organization. When the children were little, we planned it on a scale that was understandable to them and helpful to all of us. Each one was in charge of some area in which his talents could excel and also benefit the family.

Mark was in charge of all artwork, helping the rest of us with posters, etc. Kristen was our music chairman, and always accompanied anyone or assisted with her musical knowledge. Stephen was our handyman, inventor, and houseplant chairman. We could always count on him and his talent. Heidi was my kitchen assistant and a big aid to all of us. As we met each Monday evening in Family Night, we started with a business meeting to see whose talents would need to be drawn on during the week.

Now that they are all grown, some married, and all away at college, our family organization has taken on a much broader and more serious scope. *Roy* is in charge of our spiritual direction and serves as the advisor in family matters. He is always there when a newly married or recently engaged child needs to discuss something, or when one of the children need some advice in handling a personal budget, when a trying time arises in a child's occupation, a decision needs to be made in choosing classes at school, or especially when his spirit is "down" and he needs some counsel and encouragement.

I'm in charge of our knowledge and growth. This year I've assigned everyone a book to read, and we'll give reports at our next yearly meeting. I also try to see that each one continues to grow and expand his intellect whether it be through music, formal education, practical experience (such as helping in the kitchen) or study on his own. It helps me to learn also as I watch for new books, special programs, movies, lectures, or articles to pass on to them. This world is so full of fascinating things to learn about.

Stephen and his new wife, Kim, are in charge of arranging a yearly get-together; setting up schedules, a place, and a time, and so on. They also provide information for all of us on plant life since this is their field.

Mark is in charge of our genealogy and keeps us all up to date on births, death dates, pictures, etc. He also maintains his position as family artist.

Kristen and her new husband, Mark, are our finance chairmen. This is their field. (Mark was just elected vice president of finance for Brigham Young University Student Government so we feel our family funds will be in very capable hands.) We have established a family savings account with each one contributing a set amount each month. This is available to any one for use in an emergency or need. We also hope to someday be able to invest, and this will be their responsibility.

Heidi and Bruce are our food storage and preservation chairmen. They keep us up to date on new recipes, items reasonable on the market, new products, and ideas for storing and preserving and using food. Also, any health information they receive, they pass on to us.

Our family organization keeps us close in spirit though we are separated in miles, and it gives us all a feeling of security. I highly recommend it to you to try.

Life is really beautiful. Our Heavenly Father has truly made each one of us unique and special, and we become even more so as we share our lives with others.

The "pot of gold" at the end of my rainbow truly overflows as I remember the little note Steve tucked in my mailbag saying, "I love you for cutting my hair at 10:30 last night! You are the greatest!"

Or Mark as a young teenager in Sunday School on Mother's Day standing and singing "Wonderful Mother of Mine" with tears streaming down his cheeks.

Or Kristen's sweet note pinned on my pillow saying, "Thanks for staying up to fix me my favorite pancakes after work when a sandwich would have been OK. I love you with all my heart."

Or Heidi's laboriously embroidering "I love you" on a little pillow to give me as a gift when I returned from a short trip.

Roy and I sincerely hope that through the "Sunshine" of healthy living and all the colors of our family rainbow, our children will have a pot of gold to take into their new homes. Wishing them—and you—a life of Sunshine and Rainbows.

Thanks for stopping by and remember, Smile always!

Beverly's Pantry
at Sunshine Corner
Box 974
Cincinnati, Ohio 45201

So many of you have asked where you could get some of the items that I use so often, since they are not available in your stores. I'm excited to tell you I can now offer these things to you through the convenience of mail order *and* at a good price.

FOOD DEHYDRATOR

Of all the dehydrators I have worked with, the Excalibur is my Number 1 choice. It has these features:

1. Uniform air flow.
2. Fan forced thermostatically controlled air for drying.
3. Adjustable thermostat for all types of foods from herbs to jerky.
4. Nine drying trays, so simple to load and clean, should last a lifetime.
5. 17.2 sq. ft. of drying area.
6. Easy-to-remove door for simple loading.
7. 12" high x 17" deep x 22" wide.
8. One-year warranty.

It's so fast and easy to use. A lot less mess than canning food, takes up less storage space, but most important, it loses virtually no food value in the drying process. In fact, flavors are more concentrated. A dried apple slice becomes much sweeter and flavorful. For just pennies a day, you can make everything from fruit chips to meat jerky. It's the greatest for gardeners, backpackers, campers, and especially the budget conscious and those who care about the purity of their food.

I think it's *the best* buy in dehydrators at only $149.00, plus $10.00 postage and handling.

CANDY MOLDS

At last, those little mint molds you've been hunting for, made of a superior pure, pliable grey rubber material. They will last indefinitely. Since the mints pop right out of the mold, you'll only need one of each.

Shapes available—Bell, Heart, Leaf, Christmas Tree, Rose, and Swirl Mint. Why not order one of each shape and be prepared for any occasion. (Not recommended for chocolate.)

Just 99 cents each
plus 25 cents postage

PAPER CANDY CUPS

Your homemade candies look so inviting and professional when packed in individual candy cups. Stock up now and be ready for gift giving.

500 cups — only $1.25 plus 25 cents postage

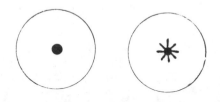

DECORATING TIPS

Be sure and order these decorating tips complete with couplers. Two tips are all you need to decorate a complete gingerbread house, hyacinth cake and many other pretty things.

Don't spend lots of money on fancy decorating kits. You'll have so much fun and much satisfaction from just these two tips.

Each tip and coupler — 79 cents plus 25 cents postage
Set of both tips and couplers — $1.50 plus 35 cents postage

DECORATING BAGS

These bags are the finest quality and easiest to use of any I've found. They wash out easily and can be used for many years of pleasure.

Each bag — $1.39 plus 25 cents postage

WHEAT GRINDER

Grind your own fresh whole wheat flour and enjoy the delicious flavor in all your baked goods.

It is so simple and clean to operate, not a speck of dust anywhere while grinding. Your flour will be as fine as baby talcum. In fact, so fine I even use mine to make "Cream Puffs." The wheat is ground between 2 carborundum stones so you are getting good, healthful, stone ground wheat with every bit of the kernel and nutrients left in.

It is entirely automatic and very easy to clean.

It can also be used for rye, rice, and cracked corn.

Has 1/6 HP motor and grinds about 5 lbs. of flour at a time.

I use mine every week and wouldn't be without it. In this age of "refined" foods, it's hard to believe how delicious some good, fresh, stone ground whole wheat flour can be in cookies, cakes, breads, or muffins.

Your family will love you and don't overlook the money you'll be saving while you all feel better too.

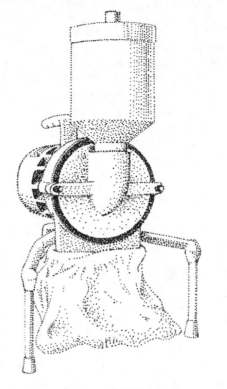

Only $110.00 plus $4.00 postage and handling

If you would like to order the best hard, red winter wheat for grinding, just let me know. The price fluctuates with the season so I'll have to send you the current prices.

It is available in large double bags or sealed storage containers and is very high in protein content and low in moisture. It is triple cleaned and is *not* chemically treated so it can be sprouted.

Just write and ask for the current wheat price and we'll send it right away.

That little kernel of wheat is DYNAMITE. Be sure and try some.

I hope these items will be as helpful and exciting for you as they have been for me and my family. In these days of inflation, we need all the help we can get, don't we? If you have any suggestions or other items you are interested in please let me know. I really appreciate all of your letters.

Smile Always,

Beverly Nye

Please send payment with order. Make check payable to Beverly's Pantry. Allow 4 weeks for delivery. Prices subject to change without notice. Ohio residents add 4 1/2 percent sales tax. Send order to:
Beverly's Pantry at Sunshine Corner
P.O. Box 974, Cincinnati, Ohio 45201

A

Antiques, our use of, 2
   refinishing, 3
   why we use, 3
Aprons, 36; pattern, 35

B

Baby, bibs, 47
   bunting, 46; pattern, 45
   burp pads, 46
   pin cushions, 47
   wrap towel, 47; illustration, 48
Baby food, choices of, 41-42
   homemade, 41-42
   keeping of, 41
Bean relish, 71
Beans, 80
Beauty aids, dried citrus rinds, 18-19
   lemon rinds, 18
   lukewarm milk, 19
   rolled oats, 19
   steam kettle, 18
Bedtimes, 133-135
Bedtime stories, 134-135
Beets, 79
Bird baths, 77
Bird feeders, 90-91
Bridal showers, 97-98
   gifts, 98-99
   invitations, 97-98
Bulbs, force-grown, 63
Bun warmer, quilted, 124; pattern, 125

C

Cake, window box, 63; pictured, 64
   flowerpot, 64

Calendar, birthday, 5-6
Camping, fire starter, 70-71
   quilts, 69
   tuna burners, 69-70
   washcloths, 69
Candles, uses of, 2-3, 70-71
Canning jars, uses of, 2
Chili, wheat, 89
Chili Relleno Casserole, Lois's, 104
Christmas decorating, 113, 116
   bell pull, 120-121
   dancing snowballs, 119-120
   kissing ball, peach pit, 120
   rose candle holder, 123; pattern, 122
   tapioca berries, 120
Christmas trees, 119
   creative ornaments, 119
   traditions with ornaments, 119
Clothesline, 78
Coconut cups, 126, 129
Cold frame, 79
Compost mixture, year-round, 90
Cookies, "He-Man," 88
Corn cobs, 85
Cranberry juice, 87
Cranberry Salad, Virginia Rowe's, 127
Crocheting, afghan, 42-43
   hangers, 43
Cucumbers, 81
Curtains, from sheets, 10

D

Diets, balanced, 19-20
Doll houses, 54; furniture for, 54
   cloth, 58
Dolls, hollyhock, 54
Dried Beef Casserole, Kristen's, 142

164 **E**

Easter, 99
Elastic, uses for, 34
Embroidery, birthday calendars, 5-6
Exercises, milk jug weights, 21
  mind, 21
  standing at sink, 20
  talking on phone, 20
  washing windows, 21
  with family, 21

F

Family Home Evening, 139-140
Family organization, 154-155
Felt book, 48; ideas for, 49-52
Fish, preparing, frying, 72
  poaching, 72
Flannel boards, 58
Fondue, 129
Food, ideas to serve youngsters, 42
Fruit trees, 78

G

Games, traveling, 74
Gardens, benefits of, 78-83
  in limited space, 78-79
  starting indoors, 79
Genealogical information, 151
Gingerbread, 114; decorating, 113, 115-116
  house pattern, 115
  icing for, 114
  variations, 95-96
Graham crackers, 89

H

Haircuts, 139
Ham, cooking method, 99-100
Hangers, crocheting, 43
  padded, 33
Happiness Notes, 20-21
Herb garden, 82-83

basil, 83
chives, 83
garlic, 83
mint, 83
mulching, 83
parsley, 83
planting, 83
Herbs, drying and uses of, 86
History, personal, 149
Holidays, personal, 95
Homemaker, role of, 1
Homemaking Day, 12
Homework, 135
Hot Cross Buns, 100; icing for, 100
Hot pads, 36

I

Ice cream, snow, 66; recipe, 65
Insect container, 67-68

J

Jams and jellies, 84-85
Journals, keeping, 149

K

Keepsake boxes, 151-153
Kraut Runzas, 136

L

Lace, trimming ideas, 98

M

Mail bag, cloth, 11-12
Mandarin Orange Salad, 143
Mehlbeutel, 99; recipe, 101
Menu planning, 42
Mexican Taco Seasoning Mix, 86
Muffins, Venna Witbeck's Bran, 140
  Pioneer Pumpkin, 128

N

Napkins, from scrap material, 11

Noodles Mexicano, 105

O

Ohio Buckeyes, 145
Orange Bubble Loaf, Sherry Jones's, 144
Orange peels, 85
Outdoor meals, 102
    preparation, fun with tablecloths,
    102-103

P

Peanut Soup, 145
Peas, 80
Picnics, 64-69
Picnic Squares, 72
Picture gallery, 6
Pictures, from print fabric, 10
    embroidery hoop types, 36-37
Pie filling, 85
Pillow, door hanging, 124; pictured, 123
    kneeling, 124
Pillowcases, personalized ideas, 123-124
Pincushions, from scrap fabric, 11
Pinking shears, 29
Pita Bread, 137; filling for, 138
Pixie game, 139
Pizza Bubbles, 144
Pizza Dough, Lauria's, 136
Place mats, from scrap fabric, 11
Pomander balls, 87
Pork Chops, Heidi's Louisiana, 141
Positive attitude, 15
Potato peels, french fried, 84
Potato Salad, 71
Prayer, 133-134
Pumpkin, cooked, 105-106
    seeds, 90

Q

Quiet book, 48; ideas for pages, 49-52
Quilting, edging, 44-45

frames, 43
tying, 43
using old nylons, 45; illustration of, 44

R

Radishes, 80; sandwiches, 80
Raisin sauce, 102
Recipes. See Index to Recipes
Rhubarb, 82; dessert, 82
Rice Krispies, bar variations, 129
    chocolate cups, 129
Root Beer, Marge's, 103
Rugs, throw, from carpet scraps, 7-8
    from double-knit scraps, 8-10
Rules for happiness and contentment, 23

S

Scones, German, 107; recipe, 106
Self-image, building in children, 152
Sewing, buttons, 32; self-covered, 32
    collars, 32
    darts, 30
    hemming, 30-31, 32-33
    hemming tape or lace, 33
    pockets, 31-32
    selecting fabric, 27, 28
    selecting style and colors, 27-28
    sleeves, 30
Sewing machine upkeep, 27
Shingle art, 5
Sleep shirts, 36
Slips, 34; tricot knit, 34, 36
Snowball Christmas Surprise, 128
Soap saver, 20
Sourdough, pancakes, 65
    starter, 65
Spices, keeping of, 11
Spice jars, used baby food jars, 11
Spinach, 80
Squash, 80
Stew, 105-106

166   Sunshine Clay, 54
      Sunshine Wheat Flakes, 88

      T

      Tin art, 4
      Toys, simple, 48, 53, 54, 55, 58-59
      Transplanting, 79
      Turkey, buying and cooking, 107-109
          pineapple decorations, 107
          pinecone name markers, 107

      V

      Valentine tree, 96-97
      Vegetable Dip, McCroby's, 81
      Vegetables, dried, uses for, 84

      W

      Wall decor, unusual, 6-7
          family talent display, 7
      Wall papering, with maps, 6-7
      White sauce, 80
      Window cleaner, 21
      Wreaths, calico ribbon, 117
          Christmas, 116-118
          dried material, 116-117
          herb, 118
          popcorn, 118

      Y

      Yams, 78-79; serving of, 102

      Z

      Zippy Carrots and Green Beans, 127

Index to Recipes

Baby food, homemade, 41
Cake, window box, 63; pictured, 64
     flowerpot, 64
Candies, Coconut cups, 126, 129
     Ohio Buckeyes, 145
     Rice Krispies, chocolate cups, 129
               bar variations, 129
Cookies, Graham Crackers, 89
     "He-Man," 88
     Picnic Squares, 72
Cranberry juice, 87
Fondue, 129
Gingerbread, 114; icing for, 114
Hot Cross Buns, 100; icing for, 100
Ice cream, snow, 65
Main dishes, Chili, wheat, 89
     Chili Relleno Casserole, Lois's, 104
     Dried Beef Casserole, Kristen's, 142
     Ham, cooking method, 99, 101
     Kraut Runzas, 136
     Mehlbeutel, 101
     Noodles Mexicano, 105
     Peanut Soup, 145
     Pita Bread, 137; filling for, 138
     Pizza Dough, Lauria's, 136
     Pork Chops, Heidi's Louisiana, 141

     Stew, 105-106
     Turkey, 108-109
Mexican Taco Seasoning Mix, 86
Muffins, Pioneer Pumpkin, 128
     Venna Witbeck's Bran, 140
Orange Bubble Loaf, Sherry Jones's, 144
Pie filling, 85
Pizza Bubbles, 144
Raisin sauce, 102
Rhubarb, 82; dessert, 82
Root Beer, Marge's, 103
Salads, Bean relish, 71
     Cranberry salad, Virginia Rowe's, 127
     Mandarin Orange Salad, 143
     Potato Salad, 71
     Zippy Carrots and Green Beans, 127
Scones, German, 106
Snowball Christmas Surprise, 128
Sourdough, pancakes, 65
     starter, 65
Sunshine Wheat Flakes, 88
Vegetable Dip, McCroby's, 81
Vegetables, Squash, 80-81
     Yams, serving of, 102
White Sauce, 80

My Favorite Recipes

My Favorite Recipes

My Favorite Recipes

My Favorite Recipes

My Favorite Recipes

My Favorite Recipes

My Favorite Recipes

My Favorite Recipes

My Favorite Recipes

My Favorite Recipes

My Favorite Recipes

My Favorite Recipes

My Favorite Recipes